Coursebook – Teacher's Edition

Book 2

A1.2

AF138072

Von	**Annie Cornford**
	Claire Hart
Herausgegeben von	**John Stevens**
Beratende Mitarbeit	**Sharon Boos**
	Christine House
	Victoria Turnbull
	Bernhard Wolff

Audios, videos, texts and interactive exercises
available on cornelsen.de/webcodes **Code: roraru**

Cornelsen

Herausgegeben von John Stevens

Im Auftrag des Verlages erarbeitet von Annie Cornford und Claire Hart

Beratende Mitwirkung
Sharon Boos, Sprockhövel; Christine House, Berlin;
Victoria Turnbull, Stuttgart; Bernhard Wolff, Hofgeismar

Redaktionsleitung
Gertrud Deutz

Projektleitung
Susanne Schütz

Redaktion (extern)
Stephanie Hempel, München
(www.redaktion-hempel.de)
Dr. Philippa Söldenwagner-Koch, Ingolstadt
(www.lektoratbilingual.de)

Redaktionelle Mitarbeit
Brianna Gorman, Christine House, Nicola Regner, Oliver Busch
(Vokabellisten)

Layoutkonzept
Rosendahl Berlin, Agentur für Markendesign

Layout und technische Umsetzung
Straive

Designberatung
Britta Scharffenberg

Umschlaggestaltung
Rosendahl Berlin, Agentur für Markendesign

Covermotiv
Bath, UK: stock.adobe.com/AlexeyFedorenko/Alexey

Illustration
Rosemarie Schöningh, Hamburg

Videos
Die Videos wurden von Wildfang, Video- und Audioprodukti-
on, Berlin im Auftrag des Cornelsen Verlages produziert.

Audios
Clarity Studio, Berlin

Basierend auf Easy English A1.2 von Annie Cornford und John Eastwood; herausgegeben von John Stevens und Christine House

www.cornelsen.de

1. Auflage, 1. Druck 2022

Alle Drucke dieser Auflage sind inhaltlich unverändert und können im Unterricht nebeneinander verwendet werden.

© 2022 Cornelsen Verlag GmbH, Berlin

Druck: Mohn Media Mohndruck, Gütersloh

ISBN 978-3-06-122710-4 (Teacher's Edition)
ISBN 978-3-06-122716-6 (Unterrichtsmanager Plus Online)
ISBN 978-3-46-420781-9 (Unterrichtsmanager Demo Version)

PEFC zertifiziert
Dieses Produkt stammt aus nachhaltig
bewirtschafteten Wäldern und kontrollierten
Quellen.

www.pefc.de

PEFC/04-31-1033

Einführung

Herzlich willkommen bei EASY ENGLISH UPGRADE! Die vorliegende TEACHER'S EDITION entspricht dem Kursbuch der Kursteilnehmenden, enthält aber hilfreiche Anmerkungen und Ergänzungen.

Das Kursbuch für die Lernenden enthält zusätzlich einen Freischaltcode für das E-Book zur Nutzung auf cornelsen.de. Für Ihren Unterricht, egal ob in Online- oder Präsenzkursen, empfehlen wir Ihnen den Unterrichtsmanager Plus mit der digitalen Version des Kursbuchs und allen Materialien zum Lehrwerk.

Das Kursbuch in der TEACHER'S EDITION gibt es zu allen sechs Bänden. So sind Sie immer gut vorbereitet – auch wenn die Zeit knapp ist. Der **Teaching Guide** mit methodischen Hinweisen, Erweiterungsvorschlägen und Kopiervorlagen ist ebenfalls ein praktischer Begleiter für Ihren Unterricht.

Was beeinhaltet die TEACHER'S EDITION**?**

- Hervorhebung von neuem Wortschatz und neuer grammatischer Strukturen
- eingedruckte Lösungen zu den Übungen
- beschriftete Fotos
- Aussprachehilfen

Das **Kursbuch** enthält 15 *Units*. Ein Dialog oder Text steht jeweils im Mittelpunkt, um den sich Wortschatz- und Grammatikarbeit, sowie Übungen zur Kommunikation drehen. Jede Unit hat eine klare Struktur mit 8 Seiten:

- Seiten 1–4: Einführung von neuem Lernstoff
- Seite 5 - SUMMARY: übersichtliche Zusammenfassung des Gelernten mit Erläuterungen zur Grammatik
- Seite 6 - FACTS & FUN: landeskundliche Hintergrundinformationen zu den Themen der *Unit*, sowie eine spielerische Zusatzaktivität.
- Seiten 7-8 EXTRA PRACTICE: Zusatzübungen für die Arbeit in der Gruppe oder zu Hause.

Jede 5. Unit ist eine CONSOLIDATION-*Unit, die* das Neu-Gelernte wiederholt und vertieft. Die sechs VIDEOS eignen sich als Modell für Dialoge und festigen den Lernerfolg Im Anschluss an eine Consolidation Unit sorgt ein MAGAZINE für Spaß und Abwechslung mit nützlichen und ungewöhnlichen Themen aus der englischsprachigen Welt.

Der **Anhang** enthält den Lösungsschlüssel, eine Grammatikübersicht und die chronologische Vokabelliste.

Alle digitalen Materialien (Audios, Videos, zusätzliche Lesetexte, Übersetzung der FACTS & FUN -Seiten) lassen sich über die kostenlose Cornelsen PagePlayer-App auf dem Smartphone oder Tablet abrufen. Alternativ lassen sich die digitalen Materialien auch unter cornelsen.de/codes herunterladen.

Viel Spaß und viel Erfolg beim Unterrichten mit EASY ENGLISH UPGRADE!

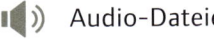 Audio-Dateien

 Video-Dateien (Filme)

 PagePlayer-App mit interaktiven Übungen,
zusätzlichen *Short Stories* und Übersetzungen von *Facts & Fun*

Contents

Grammatik	Wortschatz	Facts & Fun
• Wiederholung der einfachen Gegenwart • Wortstellung	• Arbeit und Beruf • Zeitangaben	• Taxi! • Fun with a cartoon
• Stellung der Häufigkeitsadverbien	• Jahreszeiten • Zeiträume • Besondere Tage	• Special days • Fun with a word puzzle
• *some* und *any* • Wiederholung der Fragewörter	• Im Hotel	• Unusual hotels • Fun with a word game
• Ortspräpositionen • Wiederholung: Sätze mit *there is / there are*	• Geschäfte und Einrichtungen • Denken und Wissen	• Travelling in the Outback • Fun with a puzzle
• Stellung der Häufigkeitsadverbien mit *be* • unregelmäßige Pluralformen • Bitten und Angebote mit *some* • Wiederholung: *some* und *any*	• Touristenattraktionen	

CONTENTS

Grammatik	Wortschatz	Facts & Fun
• die einfache Vergangenheit von *be*: *was, were*	• Das Wetter • Technik • Die Vergangenheit	• Nice day today? • Fun with a crossword
• die einfache Vergangenheit: regelmäßige Verben mit *-ed*	• Berufe • Verwandte • Wichtige Ereignisse	• Santa Fe, New Mexico • Silly jokes
• die einfache Vergangenheit: Verneinungen und Fragen	• Unterkunft • Landschaften • Wie etwas ist	• Welcome to Wales • Fun with the holiday game
• die einfache Vergangenheit: unregelmäßige Verben	• Tätigkeiten in der Vergangenheit • Gebäude	• Living history museums • Fun with things from the past

CONTENTS

Grammatik	Wortschatz	Facts & Fun
• Steigerung der Adjektive mit *-er, -est*	• Verkehrsmittel • am Fahrkartenschalter	• Underground travel around the world • Fun with a limerick
• Steigerung der Adjektive mit *more / most* • Steigerung von *good* und *bad*	• Kleidung • Kleidung beschreiben	• Department stores around the world • Fun with shop fronts
• Mengenangaben mit *a lot of / many / much*	• Wo man wohnt • Zimmer • Stockwerke	• Feeling at home • Fun with your perfect home
• *like / love / hate + -ing*	• Freizeitaktivitäten	• Dancing around the world • Fun with a quiz
	• Einrichtungs-gegenstände	

Appendix

1

I have two jobs

**IN DIESER UNIT
LERNEN SIE:**

- über sich, Ihren Alltag und Tagesablauf zu sprechen

01

🔊
02

Darius has two jobs. Read and listen to how he introduces himself.
Darius hat zwei Jobs. Lesen Sie und hören Sie zu, wie er sich vorstellt.

My name is Darius. I come from Iran, but I live in England now.
I have a wife, a daughter and a son.
I have two jobs, but I don't work for a company or in a shop.
I work in a care home from Monday to Friday. In the evenings, I drive a taxi.

Now introduce yourself.
Nun stellen Sie sich vor.

  My name is … and I come from …
I have … / I don't have …
I work … / I don't work.

02

Good morning!

🔊
03

Listen to Darius and repeat.
Hören Sie Darius zu und sprechen Sie nach.

Darius: I get up at six o'clock.
I start work at seven.
I don't have lunch.
I don't have a lot of free time.

Now you **03** Talk about your daily routine.

Erzählen Sie von Ihrem Tagesablauf.

		get up	
		have breakfast	in the morning.
		start work	in the afternoon.
I	(don't)	go shopping	in the evening.
		go to the gym	at … o'clock.
		have lunch	

04 Read and listen to the dialogue. Where does Darius take Olivia?

Lesen Sie den Dialog und und hören Sie zu. Wohin bringt Darius Olivia?

Answer:
to Chesterfield Road 67, an Airbnb near Manor School

Tip: Setare = [ˌsetəˈreɪ]

Darius	Good evening … can I take your bag?
Olivia	Oh, no thanks, it's not heavy.
Darius	No problem … so, where to?
Olivia	Chesterfield Road, please … number 67. It's an Airbnb near Manor School. Do you know it?
Darius	Yes, I do. My wife, Setare, is a part-time teacher there.
Olivia	That's great. Do you have children?
Darius	Yes, but they don't go to school. We have a little boy and a baby girl.
Olivia	Nice! But two small children, that's hard work! Do you work late?
Darius	I have two jobs. I don't have a lot of free time. My day job is in a care home for old people, but the money isn't very good. I work as a taxi driver every evening from eight o'clock. I finish at eleven or twelve.
Olivia	Wow, that's a busy day! For your wife too.
Darius	Yes, it's not easy but my parents live next door. They're retired, so they help on weekdays. And you?
Olivia	I'm a student teacher, but I have an interview for my first job, at Manor School.
Darius	Good luck with that … and here we are!
Olivia	Perfect, thank you so much …

Quick check **05** Circle the correct words.

Kreisen Sie die richtigen Wörter ein.

1 Darius *has* / *doesn't have* two jobs.
2 He *works* / *doesn't work* in a care home.
3 His children *go* / *don't go* to school.
4 Darius *finishes* / *doesn't finish* work early.
5 Setare's parents *help* / *don't help* with the children.
6 Darius' parents *work* / *don't work*.

06 Language

▶ Page 131

Remember: Simple present • Die einfache Gegenwart

I **work** on Friday.

Do you **work** on Sunday?

Do they **help**?

She **has** a daughter.

Does she **have** a <u>grandson</u>?

I **don't work** on Saturday.

Yes, I do. / No, I don't.

Yes, they do. / No, they don't.

She **doesn't have** a son.

Yes, she does. / No, she doesn't.

07 Make questions and answers.

Bilden Sie Fragen und Antworten.

1 Darius / drive a taxi in the morning? – No / drive a taxi in the evening

Does Darius drive a taxi in the morning?

No, he doesn't. He drives a taxi in the evening.

2 he / <u>wake up</u> at seven? – No / wake up at six.

Does he wake up at seven?

No, he doesn't. He wakes up at six.

3 Setare / <u>teach</u> every day? No / teach part-time.

Does Setare teach every day?

No, she doesn't. She teaches part-time.

EXTRA

Ask a partner two more questions.

4 the <u>grandparents</u> / help at the weekend? – No / help <u>on weekdays</u>.

Do the grandparents help at the weekend?

No, they don't. They help on weekdays.

08 Language

▶ Page 133

Word order • Wortstellung

I can come here **every day**.

He doesn't have lunch **at one o'clock**.

Do you <u>look after</u> the children **in the evening**?

09 Put the words in the correct order.
Bringen Sie die Satzteile in die richtige Reihenfolge.

1 looks after / in the evening / his wife / their children / .

   His wife looks after their children in the evening.

2 every day / Does / have brunch / she / ?

   Does she have brunch every day?

3 your son to school / in the morning / Do / take / you / ?

   Do you take your son to school in the morning?

4 doesn't / get up early / Olivia / at the weekend / .

   Olivia doesn't get up early at the weekend.

5 in the evening / Do / have a lot of free time / you / ?

   Do you have a lot of free time in the evening?

Now you ## 10 Write some questions. Use the table.
Schreiben Sie einige Fragen. Nutzen Sie die Tabelle.

	Do you	get up early?		
	Does your *(son)*			
		do at the weekend?		
		eat at lunchtime?		
Where		get up in the morning?		
What	do you	work?		
When	does your *(son)*			
What time			your	evening meal?
		have	his	lunch?
			her	*(yoga)* class?

Round up ## 11 Practise in pairs. Ask and answer the questions from exercise 10.
Üben Sie zu zweit. Befragen Sie sich gegenseitig mit den Fragen aus Übung 10.

🔴 Do you get up early?
🟣 Yes, I do. But not on Sunday.
🔴 Do you have brunch?
🟣 Only at the weekend.

Tell the class what you have learned.
Berichten Sie dem Kurs,
was Sie erfahren haben.

> Susanne gets up early, but she doesn't get up early on Sunday. She only has brunch at the weekend.

Summary

Was habe ich in dieser Unit gelernt?

COMMUNICATION

Sich vorstellen

My name is ...
I'm from Iran.
I have two jobs.
I have a daughter and a son.

Tagesablauf

My wife looks after our children in the evenings.
My parents help us on weekdays.

Berufstätigkeit

What do you do?
My day job is in a care home.
I work as a taxi driver every evening.
I finish at eleven or twelve.
My parents are both retired.
I'm a student teacher.

GRAMMAR

Wiederholung: Die einfache Gegenwart

Aussage
I **get up** early.
Darius **works** in a care home.

Verneinung
I **don't get up** late.
He **doesn't work** in an office.

Frage
Do you **get up** early?
What time **do** you **get up**?
Does Darius **work** here?
Where **does** Darius **work**?

Antwort
Yes, I do. / No, I don't.
At six o'clock.
Yes, he does. / No, he doesn't.
In a care home.

Wortstellung

Darius drives a taxi **every evening**.
I look after the children **at the weekend**.

- Die Zeitangabe, z. B. *every evening, at the weekend,* steht am Endes des Satzes und **nicht** mitten im Satz. Also **nicht** ~~Darius drives every evening a taxi~~.

VOCABULARY

Arbeit und Beruf
work
company
care home
retired

taxi driver
student teacher
interview
part-time

Zeitangaben
from Monday to Friday
in the evenings
on weekdays
at six o'clock
late

Facts & Fun

Übersetzung

05

to **stop sth** = etw (*Taxi usw.*)
anhalten

railway station = Bahnhof

for a specific time = zu einer
bestimmten Zeit

cab = Taxi

from memory = auswendig

usually = normalerweise

sth takes sb years = jd benötigt
Jahre für etw

roof = Dach

to **hail sth** = (hier:) heranwinken

sidewalk *AE* = Gehsteig

Taxi!

What can you do if you need a taxi? You can stop a taxi on the street or wait for one outside a railway station or an airport. You can phone a minicab company and book a minicab for a specific time. Or you can use an app like Uber and a car arrives very quickly.

In London, most taxis are the famous black cabs. The black cab drivers know every part of the city from memory. It usually takes them years to learn over 320 routes and 25,000 streets.

In the USA, the famous yellow cabs are a symbol of New York City. When the centre light on the car roof is on, the driver is free to take you. You "hail" a cab from the sidewalk. Just watch a New Yorker and you will see how to do it!

How do you call a taxi? Do you go on the street, make a phone call or use an app?

Fun with a cartoon

'Could you take me to the
job centre?'

Extra Practice

→ *Zusätzliche Übungen in der PagePlayer App!*

01 Match the words that go together.
Ordnen Sie die passenden Wörter einander zu.

1	watch	friends	1	*watch TV*
2	eat	a game	2	*eat a meal*
3	ask	a present	3	*ask a question*
4	play	a meal	4	*play a game*
5	meet	a question	5	*meet friends*
6	buy	TV	6	*buy a present*

02 What is Helen's daily routine? Put the sentences in the correct order.
Wie sieht Helens Tagesablauf aus? Bringen Sie die Sätze in die richtige Reihenfolge.

A   At lunchtime she has a sandwich.   **B**   Helen gets up at quarter past seven.

C   In the evening Helen <u>watches TV</u> or goes out with friends.

D   <u>Then</u> she drives to work.   **E**   She drives home at half past five.

F   She has a quick cup of coffee for breakfast.

A *4*   **B** *1*   **C** *6*   **D** *3*   **E** *5*   **F** *2*

▶ *Stellen Sie die Zeitangaben an das Satzende.*

03 Put the words in the correct order.
Bringen Sie die Satzteile in die richtige Reihenfolge.

1   at six o'clock / has / breakfast / Darius

Darius has breakfast at six o'clock.

2   at the moment / busy / is / He

He is busy at the moment.

3   at eleven or twelve / work / Darius / finishes

Darius finishes work at eleven or twelve.

4   His parents / on weekdays / their grandchildren / look after

His parents look after their grandchildren on weekdays.

5   wake up / every morning / The children / early

The children wake up early every morning.

6   doesn't drive / He / at the weekend / a taxi

He doesn't drive a taxi at the weekend.

04   What do these people do?

Was machen diese Personen beruflich?

▶ *Denken Sie daran, ein -s anzufügen, wo nötig.*

check <u>passports</u>   ~~cook in a restaurant~~   drive a taxi   look after old people

work in a <u>supermarket</u>

1   He cooks in a restaurant.   4   She works in a supermarket.

2   She drives a taxi.   5   She checks passports.

3   She looks after old people.

05   Complete the conversation.

Vervollständigen Sie das Gespräch.

David   (you / eat?) Do you eat   a big breakfast, Kyla?

Kyla   No, not often. I have a cup of coffee, but (I / not eat) I don't eat   [1]
            much.

Ben   I like a big breakfast because (I / not have) I don't have   [2] time for
            lunch. I'm always busy.

Kyla   Lisa too. (she / not have) She doesn't have   [3] time for lunch.

David   I sometimes go out at lunchtime.

Ben   Oh, (where / you / go?) where do you go?   [4]

David   The Gallery Café. (you / know) Do you know   [5] it? It's near
            the Old Art Gallery.

Kyla   (it / have) Does it have   [6] nice things on the menu?

David   Yes, it does. And (the food / not cost) the food doesn't cost   [7] much.

Tipp

Sie kochen, singen oder gärtnern gern? Dann sind Sie darin sicher auch gut. Was wir gern tun, beschert uns oft Erfolg. So auch beim Lernen: Beobachten Sie, wie Sie gern lernen. Bilder, Farben oder Tabellen sind für Sie Merkhilfen? Sie merken sich Dinge am besten, die Sie aufschreiben, oder eher das, was Sie konzentriert anhören? Mit Tests, z. B. im Internet, können Sie Ihren Lerntyp selbst ermitteln. Mehr zu diesem Thema im nächsten Tipp in Unit 3.

Happy birthday!

IN DIESER UNIT LERNEN SIE:

- die Monate und das Datum
- über Jahreszeiten und Ihren Geburtstag zu sprechen
- zu sagen, wie oft Sie in Ihrem Alltag etwas tun

Words

01
06

Complete the table. Listen and check your answers.
Vervollständigen Sie die Tabelle. Hören Sie zu und überprüfen Sie Ihre Lösungen.

Auf Englisch schreibt man *season* klein, die Monate aber groß.

spring	summer	autumn	winter
March	June	September	December
April	July	October	January
May	August	November	February

02
07

Listen and repeat.
Hören Sie zu und sprechen Sie nach.

🔴 My <u>favourite</u> <u>season</u> is autumn. <u>What about you?</u>
🟣 I don't like autumn. I like spring.
🔴 September and October are my favourite <u>months</u>.
🟣 Really? I like April and May.

Now you

03

Talk about your favourite season and your favourite months.
Sprechen Sie über Ihre Lieblingsjahreszeit und Ihre Lieblingsmonate.

🔴 My favourite season is ... . What about you?
🟣 I like ... too. I don't like ..., I like ... .

🔴 ... and ... are my favourite months.
🟣 Really? They are my favourite months too. I like ... and ....

Words **04** **Complete the table. Listen and repeat.**
08

Vervollständigen Sie die Tabelle. Hören Sie zu und sprechen Sie nach.

1**st**	first	12th	twelfth	23rd	twenty-third
2**nd**	second	13th	thirteenth	24th	twenty-fourth
3**rd**	third	14th	fourteenth	25th	twenty-fifth
4**th**	fourth	15th	fifteenth	26th	twenty-sixth
5th	fifth	16th	*sixteenth*	27th	twenty-seventh
6th	sixth	17th	seventeenth	28th	*twenty-eighth*
7th	*seventh*	18th	*eighteenth*	29th	twenty-ninth
8th	eighth	19th	nineteenth	30th	thirtieth
9th	ninth	20th	twentieth	31st	thirty-first
10th	tenth	21st	twenty-first		
11th	eleventh	22nd	*twenty-second*		

05 **Listen and repeat.**
09

Hören Sie zu und sprechen Sie nach.

 Sie schreiben: 22
August or 22nd August
Sie sagen: the twenty-
second of August

 What's the date today?
 It's the sixteenth of August.
 When's your birthday?
 It's on the twenty-second of August.

Now you **06** **Practise in pairs. Ask and answer.**

Üben Sie zu zweit. Befragen Sie sich gegenseitig.

 When's your birthday?
 My birthday is on the … of … .

07 Read and listen to the dialogue.

Lesen und hören Sie den Dialog.

10

Nick	When's your birthday, Sheila?
Sheila	It's in August. Why?
Nick	This month! When?
Sheila	On the twenty-second.
Nick	It's your birthday on the 22nd? Let's have a party. We usually do that.
Sheila	No, we don't. We sometimes have a party, but I don't like parties very much.
Nick	Why not? Birthdays are special, like Christmas or Chinese New Year …
Sheila	I know, I know. Thanks for that, Nick, but no thanks. I *really* don't like parties. OK?
Nick	OK, Sheila.

Nick	Rosie? It's Nick here. Listen, it's Sheila's birthday on Friday.
Rosie	Really? How old is she?
Nick	I never ask a woman that question! But she doesn't want a party.
Rosie	That's a pity. I like them. And I always enjoy a birthday party.
Nick	Same here. So let's have an online party. We can invite Sheila to a "special meeting" after lunch. Then I can tell our colleagues it's a surprise party.
Rosie	Oh, I don't know. People don't usually work on Friday afternoon.
Nick	I know. I often finish early too, but this is special.
Rosie	Well, OK …

Quick check ## 08 Circle the correct answers.

Kreisen Sie die richtigen Antworten ein.

1	Does Sheila like parties?	Yes, she does. /	No, she doesn't.
2	Do they sometimes have parties?	Yes, they do. /	No, they don't.
3	Does Sheila want a party?	Yes, she does. /	No, she doesn't.
4	Does Rosie always enjoy a birthday party?	Yes, she does. /	No, she doesn't.
5	Does Nick want to plan a surprise party?	Yes, he does. /	No, he doesn't.
6	Do people often finish early on Friday?	Yes, they do. /	No, they don't.

09 Language

▶ Page 134

Word order • Wortstellung

I **always** have a birthday party.

People don't **usually** work late on Fridays.

Do they **often** finish early?

We **sometimes** have brunch at the weekend.

I **never** ask a woman that question!

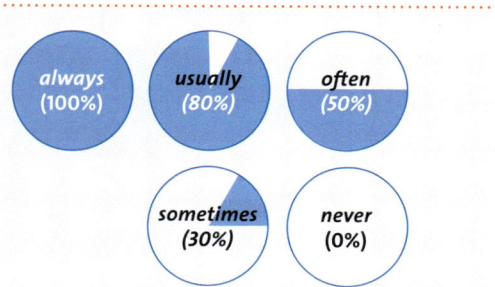

always (100%)   usually (80%)   often (50%)

sometimes (30%)   never (0%)

10 Put the word in brackets (...) in the correct place.
Setzen Sie das Wort in Klammern an die richtige Stelle.

1 Do you have online meetings? (always)

Do you always have online meetings?

2 Do you have parties with colleagues from Europe? (often)

Do you often have parties with colleagues from Europe?

3 Sheila takes a taxi from the station. (usually)

Sheila usually takes a taxi from the station.

4 I work on Saturday evening. (never)

I never work on Saturday evening.

EXTRA

Ask a partner two more questions.

5 Do you have online parties with your friends? (sometimes)

Do you sometimes have online parties with your friends?

Round up ## 11 Mark (×) what is true for you.
Kreuzen Sie an, was auf Sie zutrifft.

	always	usually	often	sometimes	never
1 I get up very early.					
2 I meet friends for lunch.					
3 I go to a vegetarian restaurant.					
4 I buy books.					
5 I swim in the winter.					
6 I go to beer gardens in the summer.					
7 I go to the cinema at the weekend.					
8 I go for a walk after lunch.					
9 I have an online party on my birthday.					
10 My family visits me on my birthday.					

 Write two sentences about yourself and read them to your partner.
Schreiben Sie zwei Sätze über sich und lesen Sie sie einander vor.

> I never swim in the winter.

> Same here. But I sometimes swim in the summer.

Was habe ich in dieser Unit gelernt?

COMMUNICATION

Die Jahreszeiten

May and June are my favourite months.
I like spring. It's my favourite season.

Das Datum

What's the date today?
It's 9 March / the ninth of March.
When is your birthday? My birthday is on the ... of ... .

Etwas bedauern

That's a pity.

Vorschläge machen

Let's have an online party.

GRAMMAR

Wortstellung

I **always** <u>go</u> out at lunchtime.
Ich gehe mittags immer aus.
Rosie **usually** <u>has</u> an online birthday party.
Rosie feiert ihren Geburtstag normalerweise online.
Sheila doesn't **often** <u>finish</u> early.
Sheila geht selten früh nach Hause.
I **sometimes** <u>work</u> late.
Ich arbeite manchmal lang.
David and Helen **never** <u>walk</u> to work.
David und Helen gehen niemals zu Fuß zur Arbeit.

* *Always, usually, often, sometimes* und *never* stehen normalerweise vor dem Verb in der einfachen Gegenwart (*buy, go, finish* usw.).
  Also **nicht**
  ~~Emma buys usually ...~~
  ~~Sheila doesn't finish often ...~~
  ~~I work sometimes ...~~
  ~~David and Helen walk never ...~~

VOCABULARY

Jahreszeiten	Zeiträume	Besondere Tage
spring	minute	birthday
summer	hour	Christmas
autumn	day	New Year
winter	week	
	month	
	year	

Übersetzung

11

Special days

to **celebrate** = feiern

Christmas Eve = Heiligabend

to **include sth** = beinhalten

special dinner = Festessen

monarch = Monarch/in

New Year's Eve = Silvester

community = Gemeinschaft

event = Ereignis

popular = beliebt

holiday = Feiertag

Tip: Eid al-fitr = [ˌiːd æl ˈfiːtəɹ]

In most English-speaking countries, people celebrate Christmas on 25th December and not on 24th December, Christmas Eve. British traditions include presents under a tree, a special dinner and the monarch on the TV.

26th December is called Boxing Day in the UK and St Stephen's Day in Ireland. The last day of the year is called New Year's Eve and it's most important in Scotland, where it is called Hogmanay.

In multi-cultural Britain, people celebrate many different special days. The biggest Muslim and Jewish communities in the UK live in London. Eid al-fitr (the end of Ramadan) is an important event in the Islamic calendar. Hanukkah, or the Jewish Festival of Lights, lasts for eight days, usually in late November and early December.

In the USA and Canada, Thanksgiving is a popular holiday in the autumn. People celebrate with their families, usually over a four-day weekend. The tradition is to give thanks for food. People cook and eat a special Thanksgiving dinner together. Which special days do you celebrate?

Fun with a word puzzle

How many special days can you find?
Wie viele Feiertage können Sie finden?

(Lösung auf Seite 157)

Z	N	N	K	H	A	N	U	K	K	A	H
K	B	E	E	A	W	J	K	S	I	T	E
D	I	W	C	H	R	I	S	T	M	A	S
O	R	Y	C	U	G	D	J	Z	L	Z	K
E	T	E	M	J	K	F	W	F	W	F	V
T	H	A	N	K	S	G	I	V	I	N	G
Q	D	R	E	I	D	A	L	F	I	T	R
P	A	X	L	P	Y	J	A	H	Y	L	W
H	Y	I	B	O	X	I	N	G	D	A	Y

Extra Practice

→ Zusätzliche Übungen in der PagePlayer App!

01 How do we say the dates? Write the words.
Wie spricht man die Daten aus? Schreiben Sie auf.

1 2 May   *the second of May*
2 23 May   *the twenty-third of May*
3 11 June   *the eleventh of June*
4 12 June   *the twelfth of June*
5 7 July   *the seventh of July*
6 30 July   *the thirtieth of July*

02 Listen to three dialogues about birthday presents. Match each dialogue with the correct picture. There is one extra picture.
12

Hören Sie sich drei Dialoge über Geburtstagsgeschenke an. Ordnen Sie jedem Dialog das passende Bild zu. Es gibt ein Bild zu viel.

A   **B**   **C**   **D**

1 *C*   **2** *A*   **3** *D*

03 Match the sentences with the responses.
Ordnen Sie die Sätze den Antworten zu.

1 Sheila always drives to work.

2 My parents often look after the baby.

3 Nick and Rosie never chat online.

4 Your husband never cooks for you.

A Yes, he does. He always makes our Christmas dinner.

B Yes, they do. They always have online meetings.

C No, they don't. They sometimes take him to the park.

D No, she doesn't. She usually walks.

1 *D*   **2** *C*   **3** *B*   **4** *A*

04

Write sentences with *always, often, sometimes* or *never*.
Schreiben Sie Sätze mit *always, often, sometimes* oder *never*.

+++ = always   ++ = often   + = sometimes   0 = never

1 Nick has lunch in the office. (++)

Nick often has lunch in the office.

2 Sheila works at weekends. (+)

Sheila sometimes works at weekends.

3 She eats out at lunchtime. (0)

She never eats out at lunchtime.

4 Nick finishes work early on Friday. (++)

Nick often finishes work early on Friday.

5 They have an online party. (+)

They sometimes have an online party.

6 Sheila enjoys parties. (0)

Sheila never enjoys parties.

7 Darius gets up early. (+++)

Darius always gets up early.

05

Complete the dialogue.
Vervollständigen Sie den Dialog.

here   idea   let's   pity   special   surprise   word

Lisa   It's Ben's birthday next Wednesday.

Kyla   OK, _____ *let's* _____ [1] have a party.

Lisa   Ben doesn't like parties much.

Kyla   That's a _____ *pity* _____ [2].

I think a birthday is a _____ *special* _____ [3] day.

Lisa   Same _____ *here* _____ [4].

Kyla   We can have a party. But don't say a _____ *word* _____ [5]

to Ben. It can be a _____ *surprise* _____ [6].

Lisa   Good _____ *idea* _____ [7].

3

I have a reservation

IN DIESER UNIT LERNEN SIE:

- in ein Hotel einzuchecken
- ein Anmeldeformular auszufüllen

01 **Daria is on a business trip in Mumbai. She checks into a hotel. Listen and repeat.**

13
Daria ist auf Dienstreise in Mumbai. Sie checkt in ein Hotel ein. Hören Sie zu und sprechen Sie nach.

Receptionist	Good afternoon. How can I help you?
Daria	I have a reservation for a single room.
Receptionist	What's your name, please?
Daria	It's Ivanova, Daria Ivanova.
Receptionist	Welcome to our hotel, Ms Ivanova. Do you have any ID?
Daria	Yes, I have my passport. Here you are.

Now you **02** **Practise the conversation with a partner.**

Üben Sie den Dialog zu zweit.

▶ *Useful language:*
single room   double room
passport   ID

- 🔴 How can I help you?
- 🟣 I have a reservation for a … room.
- 🔴 What's your name, please?
- 🟣 …
- 🔴 And do you have any ID?
- 🟣 Yes, I have my …

03 Read and listen to the dialogue. What is Daria's room number?

14

Lesen und hören Sie den Dialog. Welche Zimmernummer hat Daria?

Answer:
Room 236

Daria	Good afternoon. I have a reservation for a single room for four nights.
Receptionist	What's your name, please?
Daria	Ivanova, Daria Ivanova.
Receptionist	Welcome to our hotel, Ms Ivanova. Do you have any ID?
Daria	Yes, I have my passport and my ID card.
Receptionist	Great, thank you. Can you fill in this form for me, please?
Daria	Yes, of course. Can I pay for the room now? Do you take American Express?
Receptionist	Yes, we do. Thank you very much
Daria	Great. I don't have any Indian money. Are there any restaurants in this hotel?
Receptionist	We have a café and a bar, but we don't have any restaurants.
Daria	That's OK. Thank you. Is there free internet for guests?
Receptionist	Yes, there is. Here's your key card. You're in room 236, on the second floor. There are some lifts over there.
Daria	Thank you. And what time is breakfast?
Receptionist	It's from 6 o'clock until 10 o'clock. I see you have some luggage. Do you need any help?
Daria	No, thanks. I'm OK.

Quick check ## 04 Match the questions with the correct answers.

Verbinden Sie die Fragen mit den passenden Antworten.

1 Do you have any ID?
2 Do you take American Express?
3 Is there free internet for guests?
4 What time is breakfast?
5 Do you need any help?

A Yes, there is.
B No, thanks. I'm OK.
C It's from 6 o'clock until 10 o'clock.
D Yes, I have my passport.
E Yes, we do.

1 D   **2** E   **3** A   **4** C   **5** B

05 Language

▶ page 139

some and *any* • *some* und *any*

?	Do you have **any** ID? Are there **any** restaurants in this hotel?	Do you need **any** help?
+	I see you have **some** luggage.	There are **some** lifts over there.
–	I don't have **any** Indian money.	We don't have **any** restaurants.

06 Some or any? Circle the correct word.

Some oder *any*? Kreisen Sie das richtige Wort ein.

1 We don't have *some* / *any* Russian money.

2 I know *some* / *any* very nice hotels in Berlin.

3 Do you have *some* / *any* questions?

Now you

07 Complete the sentences and questions with *some* or *any*.

Vervollständigen Sie die Sätze und Fragen mit *some* oder *any*.

1 Excuse me. I have _some_ questions for you.

2 Are there _any_ good museums here?

3 I don't have _any_ luggage. I only have my bag.

4 Can you give us _some_ sightseeing tips, please?

5 I need _some_ coffee now. I'm very tired.

08 Language

▶ Page 132

Remember: Questions • Fragen

What's your name, please?   **Where** is the restaurant?

What time is breakfast?   **Why** do you travel to Ireland every week?

When do you clean the rooms?   **How** old is your mother?

09 Complete the questions with the correct question words.

Vervollständigen Sie die Fragen mit den richtigen Fragewörtern.

How • What • When • Where • Why

1 _What_ time is it? – It's ten o'clock.

2 _When_ do you go dancing? – At the weekend.

3 _How_ old is your daughter? – She's 11.

4 _Where_ do you buy your food? – At a supermarket.

5 _Why_ do your parents look after your children in the afternoon? –

Because I'm at work.

EXTRA

Make two more questions with how, what, when, where or why. Ask and answer the questions in pairs.

10

15

A guest checks into a hotel. Listen and mark (×) the correct answers.

Ein Gast checkt in ein Hotel ein. Hören Sie zu und kreuzen Sie die passenden Antworten an.

1 The guest's <u>surname</u> is
  A ▢ Sands.
  B ✕ Sanderson.

2 His address is
  A ✕ 112 Springhill Road, Lansley.
  B ▢ 112 Springhill Road, London.

3 A double room and breakfast costs
  A ▢ €100 a night.
  B ✕ €110 a night.

4 His room number is
  A ✕ 355.
  B ▢ 535.

5 Breakfast is
  A ▢ from 7:00 to 10:00.
  B ✕ from 7:00 to 11:00.

Round up **11**

Complete the conversation with your information and ideas.
Then practise the conversation with a partner.

Vervollständigen Sie den Dialog mit Ihren Angaben und Ideen.
Dann üben Sie den Dialog zu zweit.

Receptionist	Good afternoon. How can I help you?
Guest	I have a reservation for a *double* room for *seven* nights.
Receptionist	What's your name, please?
Guest	It's *James Sanderson*.
Receptionist	Welcome to our hotel, *Mr. Sanderson*. Do you have any ID?
Guest	Yes, I have my *passport*.
Receptionist	Great. Can I check your address?
Guest	Yes, *112 Springhill Road, Lansley, Great Britain*.
Receptionist	Do you have a credit card, *Mr. Sanderson*?
Guest	Yes, here you are.
Receptionist	Thank you. Here's your key card. Your room number is *355*. It's on the *third* floor.
Guest	Thank you. *And what time is breakfast?*
Receptionist	*It's from 7 o'clock until 11 o'clock.*
Guest	Great. Thank you.
Receptionist	You're welcome. <u>Enjoy your stay</u>!

Summary

Was habe ich in dieser Unit gelernt?

COMMUNICATION

Im Hotel einchecken

What's your name, please?
Welcome to our hotel, …
I have a reservation for a single / double room for seven nights.
Do you have any ID?
Yes, I have my passport / ID card.
Do you have a credit card?
Can you fill in this form for me, please?
Here's your key card. Your room number is …
Is there free internet / a swimming pool here?
Are there any restaurants in this hotel?
What is time is breakfast?
When is the restaurant open?
Enjoy your stay with us.

GRAMMAR

some / any

+   I have **some** luggage.
    Ich habe (etwas) Gepäck.
–   We don't have **any** single rooms.
    Wir haben keine Einzelzimmer.
?   Are there **any** good restaurants
    near here?
    Gibt es gute Restaurants in der Nähe?

We have **some** time.
Wir haben etwas Zeit.
I don't have **any** Indian money.
Ich habe kein indisches Geld.
Do you need **any** help?
Brauchen Sie Hilfe?

•   *Some* benutzt man in positiven Aussagen (+), *any* in Verneinungen (–)
    und Fragen (?).

Wiederholung: Fragewörter

What time is breakfast?
Wann gibt es Frühstück?
Where is the hotel?
Wo ist das Hotel?
When is the next train?
Wann fährt der nächste Zug?

What's your name, please?
Wie heißen Sie?
Why do you get up early?
Warum stehst du so früh auf?
How can I help you?
Wie kann ich Ihnen helfen?

VOCABULARY

Im Hotel

breakfast
to check in
to check out
credit card
form
ID (card)

key card
passport
payment
luggage
reservation

Facts & Fun

Übersetzung

16

unusual = außergewöhnlich, ausgefallen

normally = normalerweise

gym = Fitnessraum

wall = Wand

furniture = Möbel

hot tub = Warmwasserbecken

sleeping bag = Schlafsack

to **prefer sth** = etw bevorzugen

to **try sth** = etw ausprobieren

massive = riesig

to **swim by** = vorbeischwimmen

Unusual hotels

When you think of a hotel, you normally think of a big building in a city or near the sea with a lot of bedrooms. There's usually a restaurant, a swimming pool and maybe a gym. But not all hotels are the same.

In an ice hotel, the walls of the building and all the furniture are made of blocks of ice and snow. You can find ice hotels in countries with low temperatures in winter, like Finland and Iceland. Some ice hotels have bars, saunas and hot tubs. Temperatures in the bedrooms are usually below 0 degrees Celsius. Guests wear warm clothes all the time and sleep in sleeping bags on beds made of ice.

If you prefer something warmer and more tropical, try an underwater hotel. Sometimes these hotels are under the sea in places like the Maldives. Some of these hotels are far from the sea in the middle of a city, like Shanghai, but the rooms are inside a massive aquarium. The guests can watch the fish swim by from their beds!

What type of hotels do you like?

Fun with a word game

How many words can you make from the letters of the hotel?
Wie viele Wörter können Sie aus den Buchstaben des Hotels bilden?

(Lösung auf Seite 157)   *in, lot, can, ace, act, arc, car, can't, cola, continent, hotel etc.*

Extra Practice

➜ *Zusätzliche Übungen in der PagePlayer App!*

01 Make words and then match them to the German translations.
Bilden Sie Wörter und ordnen Sie sie den deutschen Übersetzungen zu.

~~after~~	code	1	*afternoon*	A Enkel
break	end	2	*breakfast*	B Frühstück
grand	fast	3	*grandson*	C Nachmittag
pass	man	4	*passport*	D Polizist
police	~~noon~~	5	*policeman*	E Pass
post	port	6	*post code*	F Wochenende
week	son	7	*weekend*	G Postleitzahl

02 What do you see in the pictures? Write *a* or *some* and the correct word. Sometimes you need to add *-s*.
Was sehen Sie in den Bildern? Benutzen Sie *a* oder *some* und das entsprechende Wort. Manchmal müssen Sie ein *-s* anfügen.

bottle   chip   cup   glass   key   luggage   soup   dress   wine

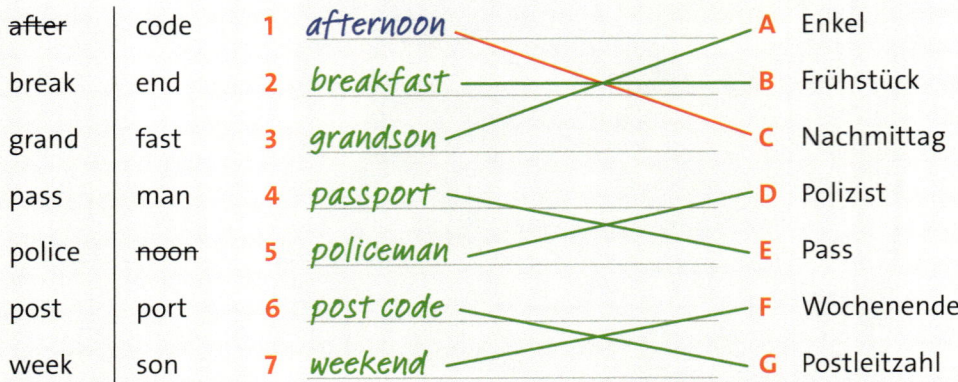

1	*a cup*	4	*a dress*	7	*a glass*
2	*some chips*	5	*some wine*	8	*some luggage*
3	*some soup*	6	*some bottles*	9	*some keys*

03 Match the hotel words with the correct sentences.
Ordnen Sie die Hotel-Wörter den richtigen Sätzen zu.

1 check-out   A When you <u>leave</u> the hotel.
2 key card   B This has your name and other <u>information</u> on it.
3 ID card   C You write your name and other information on it.
4 luggage   D The clothes and other things you take to a hotel.
5 form   E You use it to go into your room.

1 *A*   **2** *E*   **3** *B*   **4** *D*   **5** *C*

04 Put the words in the correct order and make questions.
Bringen Sie die Wörter in die richtige Reihenfolge und bilden Sie Fragen.

1 breakfast / is / the / room? / Where

Where is the breakfast room?

2 cards? / credit / Do / take / you

Do you take credit cards?

3 a / Is / here? / sauna / there

Is there a sauna here?

4 a bus / from / here? / Is / or / there / train

Is there a bus or train from here?

5 is / next / the / time / train? / What

What time is the next train?

6 cost? / does / How / much / a taxi

How much does a taxi cost?

05 Circle the correct words.
Kreisen Sie die passenden Wörter ein.

Receptionist Good evening. Welcome in / *to* the Queen's Hotel. *How* / What can I help you?

Anton I *has* / *have* a reservation for a *one* / *only* / *single* room.

Receptionist *How's* / *What's* your name, please?

Anton Brown. Anton Brown.

Receptionist *Do* / *Does* you have any ID, please?

Anton Yes, I have my passport. Here you are.

Receptionist That's fine. Thank you. Here's your key card. Your room number is 218. It's on the third *ground* / *floor*.

Anton Thanks. *What* / *When* time is breakfast?

Receptionist Breakfast is *from* / *at* 7 o'clock until 10 o'clock. There are *any* / *some* breakfast menus here.

Anton Thank you.

Receptionist You're welcome. Enjoy *you* / *your* stay with us.

TIPP

Finden Sie heraus, wie Sie Vokabeln am besten lernen. Teilen Sie den Wortschatz einer Unit in Pakete mit maximal sieben Wörtern ein und lernen Sie jedes Paket auf andere Weise. Schreiben Sie die Wörter z. B. so untereinander, dass ihre Anfangsbuchstaben ein seltsames Wort ergeben. Oder verknüpfen Sie jedes Wort mit einem Bild, oder verbinden Sie die Wörter durch eine kurze Geschichte. Mit welcher Technik behalten Sie die meisten Wörter?

Go along this road

IN DIESER UNIT LERNEN SIE:

- nach dem Weg zu fragen
- Wegbeschreibungen zu geben

01 Rodrigo asks the way at the reception in his hotel. Listen and repeat.

17

Rodrigo fragt am Empfang seines Hotels nach dem Weg.
Hören Sie zu und sprechen Sie nach.

Rodrigo   Is there a bank near here?
Receptionist   Yes, there is. Go out of the hotel. Turn right.
Go along York Road. There's a pub on the right.
Turn left into Park Street. Go along Park Street.
The bank is on the left.

Words 02 Listen and repeat.

18

Hören Sie zu und sprechen Sie nach.

Go straight on.
The supermarket is on the corner.
It's next to the pub.
It's opposite the church.

Now you 03 Practise in pairs. You are in the hotel. Ask where the post office is and where a café is. Then tell your partner the way.

Üben Sie zu zweit. Sie sind im Hotel. Fragen Sie nach der Post und einem Café.
Dann erklären Sie Ihrem Partner / Ihrer Partnerin den Weg.

 Is there a … near here?
 Yes, there is.

Go straight on.   There's a … on the …   Go along …
Turn …   Turn left into …   And the … is on the …

Now you **04**

Read and listen to the dialogue. Where does Rodrigo want to go now?

Lesen Sie den Dialog und hören Sie zu. Wo will Rodrigo jetzt hin?

19

Answer:
To the cash machine

Rodrigo	Good morning. Is there a cash machine near here?
Receptionist	Yes, there is. On Park Street.
Rodrigo	Can you tell me the way, please?
Receptionist	Yes, of course. Go out of the hotel and turn right. Go along York Road. There's a pub on the right. It's the White Lion. Turn left into Park Street.
Rodrigo	So that's left into Park Street.
Receptionist	Yes. Go along Park Street. The cash machine's on the left. It's next to a bookshop.
Rodrigo	Great. And is there a pharmacy too?
Receptionist	Yes, there is. It's on Park Street. Go straight on at the traffic lights. The pharmacy is on the corner, opposite the newsagent's.
Rodrigo	Great, thanks. Is it far?
Receptionist	No, it's about ten minutes from here. Would you like a map?
Rodrigo	Yes. Thanks very much.

Quick check **05** **Are the sentences true (T) or false (F)? Mark (✗) the correct box.**

Sind die Sätze richtig (T) oder falsch (F)? Kreuzen Sie an.

	T	F	
1	✗		There is a cash machine near the hotel.
2		✗	The White Lion pub is on the corner of Green Street and York Road.
3	✗		The cash machine is next to a bookshop on York Road.
4		✗	The newsagent's is opposite the bookshop.
5		✗	The pharmacy is next to the newsagent's.

06 **Language**

Where things are • Wegbeschreibungen

Go **out of** the hotel.
Go straight on **at** the traffic lights.
Go **along** York Road.
Turn left **into** Park Street.

It's **next to** a bookshop.
It's **opposite** the pharmacy.
The art gallery is **near** here.

07 Complete the sentences.
Vervollständigen Sie die Sätze.

into • at • near • of • on (3 x) • opposite • to

1. Is there a post office *near* here?
2. Turn left into Old Street and go straight *on*.
3. There's a pub *on* the right.
4. The café is next *to* the phone shop.
5. Turn left *at* the traffic lights.
6. There's a nice bar *on* the corner.
7. Go out *of* the hotel.
8. The bookshop is *opposite* the bank.
9. Turn right and go *into* South Street.

08 A hotel guest wants to go to places A, B and C on the map. Listen and write A, B or C in the boxes.
🔊 20

Ein Hotelgast will zu den Orten A, B und C. Hören Sie zu und tragen Sie A, B oder C in die Kästchen ein.

1 *B* train station   **2** *C* cinema   **3** *A* supermarket

09 Language

Remember: is / are

Is there a bank near here?

There's a bank on Park Street.

Are there any nice shops here?

There are some good pubs.

Yes, **there is.** / No, **there isn't.**

There isn't a bank on York Road.

Yes, **there are.** / No, **there aren't.**

There aren't any good pubs.

10 Make questions.
Bilden Sie Fragen.

	good hotel	
	train station	
Is there a	Irish pub	
Is there an	cash machine	near here?
Are there any	pharmacy	
	supermarkets	
	night buses	

Now you

11 Practise with a partner. Ask the questions from exercise 10. Answer the questions with short answers. Give more information if you can.
Üben Sie zu zweit. Stellen Sie die Fragen aus Übung 10. Beantworten Sie die Fragen mit Kurzantworten. Machen Sie nach Möglichkeit weitere Angaben.

Yes, there is. • Yes, there are. • No, there isn't. • No, there aren't.

> Is there a good hotel near here?

> Yes, there is. The Mühle in Mühlenstraße.

Round up

12 Choose a place near to your language school.
Ask your partner for directions to this place.
Wählen Sie einen Ort in der Nähe von Ihrer Sprachschule.
Fragen Sie, wie Sie zu Ihrem Ziel kommen.

- 🔴 Excuse me. Is there a *(pharmacy)* near here?
- 🟣 Yes, there is. *(In Hauptstraße)*.
- 🔴 Can you tell me the way from here?
- 🟣 Yes, of course. Go out of the language school. Turn …

Summary

Was habe ich in dieser Unit gelernt?

COMMUNICATION

Nach dem Weg fragen

Is there a supermarket near here?
Can you tell me the way to a cash machine, please?
Is it far?

Wegbeschreibungen

Go along this street.
Go straight on.
Turn right / left at the traffic lights.
There's a hotel on the right / left.
The supermarket is on the right / left.
It's next to / opposite / near the bookshop.
It's five minutes from here.

GRAMMAR

Wo und wohin?

There's a pub **near** the train station.
Es gibt eine Kneipe in der Nähe des Bahnhofs.

The pharmacy is **next to** the bookshop.
Die Apotheke ist neben der Buchhandlung.

It's **opposite** a newsagent's.
Sie ist gegenüber von einem Zeitungsladen.

Go **out of** the station.
Gehen Sie aus dem Bahnhof hinaus.

Turn left **at** the traffic lights.
Biegen Sie an der Ampel links ab.

Go **along** East Street.
Gehen Sie die East Street entlang.

Go **into** the park.
Gehen Sie in den Park.

The café is **on** the left, **on** the corner.
Das Café ist auf der linken Seite, an der Ecke.

Wiederholung: Sätze mit *there is / there are*

There's a train station.
There are buses.
Is there a theatre?
Are there any good museums?

There isn't an airport.
There aren't any night buses.
Yes, **there is.** / No, **there isn't.**
Yes, **there are.** / No, **there aren't.**

VOCABULARY

Geschäfte und Einrichtungen
cash machine
newsagent's
pharmacy
supermarket
shopping centre
train station

Denken und Wissen
think
remember
know (= *wissen*)
know (= *kennen*)

Facts & Fun

Übersetzung

🔊
21

feeling = Gefühl

to agree = sich einig sein

square = Quadrat-

size = Größe

up-to-date = aktuell

petrol = Treibstoff

tool = Werkzeug

to fix a problem = ein Problem
beheben

first aid kit = Erste-Hilfe-Kasten

dangerous = gefährlich

snake = Schlange

spider = Spinne

Travelling in the Outback

Some Australians say the Outback is a place. Other Australians say it's a feeling that you are far from any towns or houses. Everybody agrees that the Outback is in the middle of Australia and that it's millions of square kilometres in size. Only about 700,000 people live there today. A lot of people in the Outback live very far from a school or a hospital, most children learn at home and doctors fly around the Outback in small planes to help people. These doctors are called 'flying doctors'.

When you travel in the Outback, take a very good and up-to-date map with you! Take a lot of food and water too. There are no buses or trains in the Outback so take some extra petrol and some tools. Then you can fix any problems with your car. It's a good idea to take a first aid kit with you too. There are some dangerous animals, like crocodiles, snakes and spiders, out there!

Fun with a puzzle

Auf dem Stadtplan sind acht Gebäude in der Victoria Street eingezeichnet. Die Lage des *bookshop* ist angegeben. Wo befinden sich die anderen Gebäude?

- The bookshop is on the corner.
- The pharmacy is opposite the café.
- The post office is next to the cinema.
- The cash machine is on the corner.
- The pub is opposite the post office and next to the newsagent's.
- The café is **not** next to the post office.
- The cinema is next to the bookshop.

(Lösung auf Seite 157)

Extra Practice

→ *Zusätzliche Übungen in der PagePlayer App!*

01 Where are the buildings? Complete the sentences.
Wo stehen die Gebäude? Vervollständigen Sie die Sätze.

1 The hotel *is on the right. It's next to the supermarket.*

2 The art gallery *is on the left. It's next to the museum.*

3 The theatre *is on the left. It's next to the swimming pool.*

4 The bookshop *is on the right. It's next to the pharmacy.*

02 Noor is in the shop. Look at the town plan and complete Noor's conversation with a shop assistant.
Noor ist im Laden. Sehen Sie sich den Stadtplan an und vervollständigen Sie Noors Dialog mit der Verkäuferin.

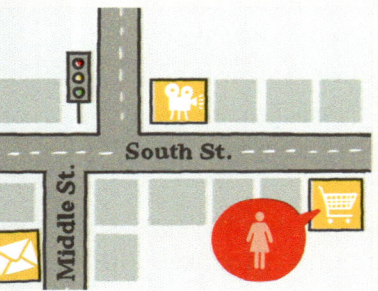

Noor Can you tell me the _____*way*_____ [1] to the post office, please?

Assistant Yes, it isn't _____*far*_____ [2] from here. Go _____*straight*_____ [3] and turn _____*left*_____ [4]. Go _____*down*_____ [5] the street. There's a _____*cinema*_____ [6] on the right. Go _____*straight*_____ [7] on and then at the _____*light*_____ [8] turn _____*left*_____ [9] into _____*Middle*_____ [10] Street. The post office is on the _____*right*_____ [11].

Noor Thank you.

03 Match the German sentences with the correct English sentences.
Ordnen Sie die deutschen Sätze den passenden englischen Sätzen zu.

1 Ich bin im Urlaub.
2 Ich bin sehr beschäftigt.
3 Darf ich eine Frage stellen?
4 Ich auch.
5 Ich habe eine Reservierung.
6 Können Sie mir sagen, wie ich dahin komme?

A Can I ask a question?
B Can you tell me the way?
C I have a reservation.
D I'm on holiday.
E I'm very busy.
F Me too.

1 *D* **2** *E* **3** *A* **4** *F* **5** *C* **6** *B*

04 Complete the sentences. Use words from this unit.
Vervollständigen Sie die Sätze. Benutzen Sie Wörter aus dieser Unit.

1 You need some *money?*   Go to *a bank.*

2 You need a nice *meal?*   Go to *a restaurant.*

3 You need *a drink?*   Go to *a pub.*

4 You need an *oyster card?*   Go to *the station.*

05 Write sentences with *There are ...*
Schreiben Sie Sätze mit *There are ...*

1 seasons / year   *There are four seasons in a year.*

2 hours / day   *There are 24 hours in a day.*

3 months / year   *There are twelve months in a year.*

4 days / March   *There are thirty-one days in March.*

06 Solve the crossword puzzle.
Lösen Sie das Kreuzworträtsel.

→
1 I'm usually ... home on Sunday.
2 I go dancing ... my wife.
3 It's ten minutes ... here.
6 Is there a bank ... here?
8 I look after the children ... the morning.
9 A glass ... milk, please.
10 Go ... of the building and turn right.
11 Do you often go ... the theatre?

↓
1 I sing in the choir ... work.
3 This is a present ... you.
4 The concert is ... 16 October.
5 Turn right ... North Street.
6 The bank is ... to the supermarket.
7 What ... a pub lunch? – Good idea.

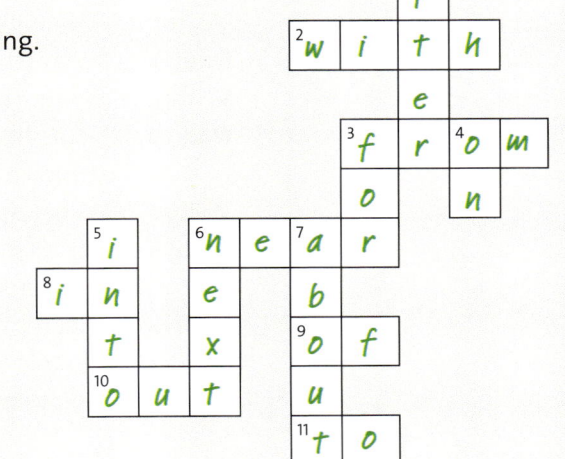

Consolidation

5

In dieser Unit wird das Wichtigste aus Units 1 bis 4 wiederholt und vertieft.

AUSSERDEM LERNEN SIE:

- *always, usually* usw. mit *am, is* und *are*
- einige unregelmäßige Pluralformen
- *some* in Angeboten und Bitten

01

22

Read and listen to a dialogue at a tourist information centre in Bristol. Explain how you can go from the city centre to the fiesta.
Lesen und hören Sie einen Dialog in einer Touristeninformation in Bristol. Erklären Sie, wie man von der Stadtmitte zur Fiesta kommt.

Answer:
You can take a special bus from the centre to the fiesta at ten past eleven.

Visitor	Are there any interesting events near here?
Nadiya	Yes, the famous balloon fiesta, for example.
Visitor	Oh really? When does it start?
Nadiya	It starts today and ends on 12th August – on Sunday.
Visitor	Where is it?
Nadiya	Outside the city, but it's only two miles from here. There are special buses from the centre to the fiesta.
Visitor	When is the next bus?
Nadiya	It's at ten past eleven.
Visitor	How much does the fiesta cost?
Nadiya	Oh, it's free. It's always very popular. There are usually half a million people there.
Visitor	OK, thank you.

Quick check **02** Are the sentences true (T) or false (F)? Mark (✗) the correct box.

Sind die Sätze richtig (T) oder falsch (F)? Kreuzen Sie an.

	T	F	
1	✗		The balloon fiesta is famous.
2	✗		It's two miles from the tourist office to the fiesta.
3		✗	There is a bus at 10:11.
4		✗	The fiesta costs £12.
5	✗		A lot of people go to the fiesta.

03 **Language**

▶ Page 134

Word order: *am / is / are* + *always, usually, never*

The fiesta is **always** very popular.

There are **usually** half a million people there.

Remember **Word order: *always, usually, never* + verb**

I **always** enjoy the fiesta.

We **usually** go there in the evening.

04 Put the words in the correct order and make sentences.

Bringen Sie die Wörter in die richtige Reihenfolge und bilden Sie Sätze.

1 always / The fiesta / is / very good

The fiesta is always very good.

2 eat / often / People / on the waterfront

People often eat on the waterfront.

3 The bus / is / late / often

The bus is often late.

4 the fiesta / I / on TV / usually / watch

I usually watch the fiesta on TV.

5 early / is / never / That train

That train is never early.

6 always / The food / good / here / is

The food is always good here.

EXTRA

Write sentences with always, usually and never about you and your life.

05 When are these events? Write sentences.

Wann finden diese Veranstaltungen statt? Schreiben Sie Sätze.

1 Yoga is on the ninth of May at a quarter to eight.

2 The concert is on the eighteenth of March at half seven.

3 The city tour is on the twenty-third of July at quarter past nine.

4 The cocktail party is on the second of August at half past six.

06 Listen and repeat the singular and plural nouns.

23

Hören Sie zu und sprechen Sie die Singular- und Pluralformen nach.

one person → two people   one woman → two women
one man   → five men   one child → some children

07 Complete the sentences with the plural forms of the words.

Vervollständigen Sie die Sätze mit den Pluralformen der Wörter.

1 There's an interesting museum for _____ *children* _____ here. (child)

2 There are a lot of _____ *people* _____ in the bookshop. (person)

3 The _____ *women* _____ are all in the pub. (woman)

4 The _____ *men* _____ are on the bus. (man)

08 Read and listen to another dialogue at the tourist information centre. What information do the leaflets give?

24

Lesen und hören Sie einen weiteren Dialog in der Touristeninformation. Welche Informationen beinhalten die Broschüren?

Answer:
Information about
attractions in the city

Visitor Excuse me. Do you have a map of the city?

Nadiya Yes, I think so. Where are they? … Oh no, we don't have any maps. We usually have some, but … Oh yes, here they are. Sorry.

Visitor Thank you. And can I ask about buses …?

Nadiya Buses … buses … Oh yes, here is some information about buses. And here's a timetable. It has the times of all the buses. And would you like some leaflets about attractions in the city?

Visitor Yes, please. Thank you very much.

09 Language

▶ Page 139

some

Would you like **some** leaflets? *(Angebot)*

Can I have **some** leaflets, please? *(Bitte)*

Remember **some / any**

+	positive	There are **some** maps. There is **some** information.
–	negative	There aren't **any** maps. There isn't **any** information.
?	question	Are there **any** maps? Is there **any** information?

10 Complete the sentences with *some* or *any*.
Vervollständigen Sie die Sätze mit *some* oder *any*.

1 Are there _____*any*_____ hotels near here?

2 We have _____*some*_____ information about trains here.

3 Would you like _____*some*_____ help with your bag?

4 Do you know _____*any*_____ good cafés or restaurants?

5 There aren't _____*any*_____ maps here.

6 I have _____*some*_____ questions about the theatre.

Round-up ## 11 Match the questions with the correct answers. Then complete the answers with information about your town or city.
Verbinden Sie die Fragen mit den passenden Antworten. Dann vervollständigen Sie die Antworten mit Informationen über Ihre Stadt.

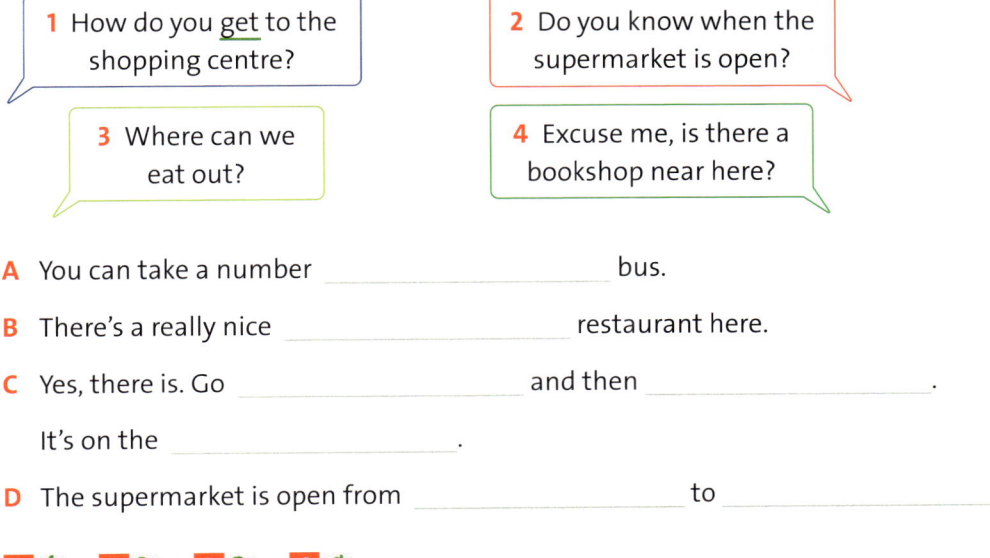

1 How do you get to the shopping centre?

2 Do you know when the supermarket is open?

3 Where can we eat out?

4 Excuse me, is there a bookshop near here?

A You can take a number _____ bus.

B There's a really nice _____ restaurant here.

C Yes, there is. Go _____ and then _____.
  It's on the _____.

D The supermarket is open from _____ to _____.

1 *A*   **2** *D*   **3** *B*   **4** *C*

Review

1. Sehen Sie sich Vanessas Terminkalender an. Sagen Sie, was Vanessa wann und wie oft vorhat.

Monday	Tuesday	Wednesday	Thursday	Friday
Start work at 8 o'clock and finish work at 3 o'clock	Start work at 8 o'clock and finish work at 4 o'clock	Go to a yoga class at 10:30	Start work at 8 o'clock and finish work at 4 o'clock	Start work at 7 o'clock and finish work at 1 o'clock
Look after my sister's daughter in the afternoon	Do the shopping		Have lunch with Mary	Play tennis in the afternoon

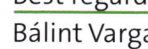

2. Nennen Sie Ihre Lieblingsjahreszeit und nennen Sie zwei Daten, die für Sie wichtig sind.

3. Sie haben ein Hotelzimmer für eine Dienstreise gebucht. Lesen Sie die E-Mail-Bestätigung, die Sie bekommen haben. Erfinden Sie allein oder mit einer Partnerin/einem Partner ein Rollenspiel über Ihre Ankunft an der Rezeption.

Dear Mr/Ms ... ,

Thank you for your reservation at the Grand Palace Hotel, Budapest.
We can confirm your booking for one single room for five nights from 14th March until 19th March.
The cost of this room is 79 euros a night.
There is free internet for all guests and breakfast is included in the price of the room. Breakfast is from 7 a.m. until 10:30 a.m. in our restaurant.

Best regards,
Bálint Varga
Reception team, Grand Palace Hotel Budapest

Town Centre

4. Üben Sie zu zweit. Fertigen Sie eine Karte Ihrer Stadt an und zeichnen Sie fünf Orte ein. Beschreiben Sie den Weg von einem Ort zum anderen.

Videos

01 Visiting Cornwall

01

Cornwall is a beautiful part of south west England. It is very popular with British tourists and has many visitors from other parts of the world too. What's it like there? Watch the video and answer the questions.

Mark (✗) the correct answer.

1 How many people in Cornwall speak the Cornish language today?
A ▢ a lot of them B ▢ most of them
C ✗ very few of them

2 What has an enormous impact on life in Cornwall?
A ▢ artists and writers B ✗ the sea
C ▢ the tin mines

3 What did the Cornish tin miners take for their lunch in the past?
A ✗ pasties B ▢ cream teas
C ▢ local seafood

4 Where can you sit outside and watch a play or an opera?
A ▢ Tintagel Castle B ▢ Lands End
C ✗ the Minack

 What did you already know about Cornwall? Now watch the video again. What did you learn from the video? Would you like to go there? Talk about what you would like to see and do if you visit Cornwall one day.

02 Checking into the hotel

02

It's the start of the Games Industry Convention, and Enrico Rossi has a reservation at a hotel in the city. Watch the video and answer the questions.

1 The hotel receptionist asks for ID. What does Enrico give him?
2 Where does Enrico come from and where did he learn to speak English?
3 What time does the hotel kitchen open for lunch on weekdays?
4 What is Enrico's room number and what floor is it on?
5 The receptionist gives Enrico a form to write his address and contact details. What other information does he ask for?
6 Enrico writes a note for a guest called S Newton. What happens to the note?

 Watch the video again. Talk about why Enrico is not very happy about the hotel kitchen. Where can he get some breakfast?

Bristol and Bath Scrapbook

CLIFTON SUSPENSION BRIDGE

Bristol is a fantastic city. The engineer Isambard Kingdom Brunel designed the Clifton Suspension Bridge 150 years ago. You can walk or drive across it and see the River Avon far below. The bridge is a symbol of Bristol.

BRISTOL HARBOURSIDE

Two hundred years ago, this was the port of Bristol. The slave trade as well as the tobacco trade made the city very rich. Today there are art galleries, shops, wine bars and restaurants here. There's a cultural centre and an interactive science museum – a big hit with children.

STREET ART IN BRISTOL

There's a lot of street art in Bristol. Many years ago, Nelson Street was not very interesting, but today it is the home of one of the UK's biggest street art projects. The street artist Banksy comes from Bristol, and you can see his art in some places in the city.

A LITTLE HELP:

- **scrapbook** Sammelalbum
- **suspension bridge** Hängebrück
- **designed by** entworfen von
- **engineer** Ingenieur/in
- **river** Fluss
- **below** unten
- **harbourside** Hafengelände
- **slave trade** Sklavenhandel
- **tobacco trade** Tabakhandel
- **port** Hafen
- **science** Naturwissenschaften
- **artist** Künstler/in

PULTNEY BRIDGE

A twenty-minute train ride from Bristol takes you to the smaller city of Bath Spa. Its famous bridge over the River Avon was built in 1773 and has shops on both sides, as in some Italian cities.

ELEGANT BUILDINGS

The city is famous for its iconic 18th century architecture and the honey-coloured Bath stone. The Royal Crescent is a grand row of thirty terraces, which look out across Victoria Park. One of these terraces is a luxury hotel.

THE ROMAN BATHS

Of course, on a visit to Bath Spa, you mustn't miss the Roman Baths. They were built around 70 AD and are one of the best preserved Roman ruins in the world. Hot spring water, up to 46°C, still fills the baths every day. Actors in Roman costumes can take you back to that ancient world, or you can have fun in the interactive museum.

A LITTLE HELP:

- **iconic** ikonenhaft, kultig
- **honey-coloured** honigfarben
- **stone** Stein
- **row** Reihe
- **preserved** erhalten
- **spring water** Quellwasser
- **ancient world** Antike

6 That long, hot summer

IN DIESER UNIT LERNEN SIE:

• über das Wetter zu sprechen
• über Ihre Erinnerungen zu sprechen

Words

01
🔊 25

Match the words with the pictures. Then listen, check your answers and repeat.
Ordnen Sie die Wörter den Bildern zu. Dann hören Sie zu, überprüfen Sie Ihre Lösungen und sprechen Sie nach.

1    **2**    **3**    **4**    **5**    **6**

| A | cold | C | sunny | E | wet |
| B | hot | D | warm | F | windy |

1 A   **2** D   **3** B   **4** C   **5** F   **6** E

02
🔊 26

Bonnie meets her old friend Sam in a bar in Bristol. Listen and repeat.
Bonnie trifft sich mit Sam, einem alten Freund, in einer Bar in Bristol. Hören Sie zu und sprechen Sie nach.

Sam   It's a lovely evening.
Bonnie   Yes, it is. It's nice today.
Sam   But it was cold yesterday.
Bonnie   You're right, it was awful last night.

Now you **03** Talk about the weather.

Sprechen Sie über das Wetter.

▶ *Useful language:*
lovely   awful
nice   not very nice
great   not so good

💬 It's a / an … day / morning / afternoon / evening.
💬 Yes, it is. It's … today.
💬 It was … yesterday too. / But it was … yesterday.
💬 Yes, you're right, it was …

04 Read and listen to the dialogue. When were the good old days? 3, 6 or 12 years ago?

27

Lesen und hören Sie den Dialog. Wann waren die guten alten Zeiten? Sind sie 3, 6 oder 12 Jahre her?

Answer:
Twelve years ago

Sam	It's a great evening.
Bonnie	Yes, it is. It's nice today.
Sam	But it was cold yesterday.
Bonnie	You're right, it was awful last night.
Sam	It's lovely on the waterfront now. I remember, there was only one little café.
Bonnie	Yes, it wasn't very nice here twelve years ago. There weren't many bars here then, but now it's the best place in town.
Sam	Was it really twelve years ago?
Bonnie	Yes, it was! We were both new in town then.
Sam	It was that long hot summer. Do you remember?
Bonnie	Were the days really always sunny when we were young?
Sam	No, of course they weren't!
Bonnie	But life was different then.
Sam	You were with William.
Bonnie	That's right. We were married for six years. I'm divorced now.
Sam	Yes, I know. When was that?
Bonnie	Three years ago. Where were you then?
Sam	I was in Hong Kong, then in Dubai. I'm back in the States now, in L.A.
Bonnie	Are you happy in America? Do you miss England?
Sam	I don't miss the rain or the cold houses. But I miss some things …
Bonnie	Let's have some more wine. We can drink to the good old days!
Sam	Sure. Why not?

Quick check **05** Circle the correct words.

Kreisen Sie die richtigen Wörter ein.

1 The weather *(was)* / *wasn't* cold in Bristol yesterday.

2 There *were* / *(weren't)* many bars there twelve years ago.

3 Bonnie and Sam *(were)* / *weren't* both new in town then.

4 Bonnie *was* / *(wasn't)* married to Sam.

5 Sam *was* / *(wasn't)* in America three years ago.

06 Language

▶ Page 135

The simple past: *was / were* • Die einfache Vergangenheit: *was / were*

I / He / She **was** in Bristol last year.	I / He / She **wasn't** in L. A..
It **was** cold yesterday.	It **wasn't** a nice day.
There **was** only one little café.	There **weren't** many bars.
You **were** with William.	You **weren't** married then.
We / They **were** young.	We / They **weren't** old.
Was she happy?	Yes, she **was.** / No, she **wasn't.**
Were they happy?	Yes, they **were.** / No, they **weren't.**

07 Complete the sentences.
Vervollständigen Sie die Sätze.

EXTRA

Make two more sentences that are true for you. Use was / were *or* wasn't / weren't.

was • wasn't • were • weren't

1 It _____was_____ very warm yesterday, it wasn't cold.

2 People always say that the summers _____were_____ better in the good old days.

3 Who _____was_____ that girl that you _____were_____ with last night?

4 You _____weren't_____ in London last week, you were in Liverpool!

5 _____Was_____ your friend at a party last weekend? – No, he _____wasn't_____ .

6 _____Were_____ your trains late on Monday? – Yes, but they _____weren't_____ late

on Tuesday.

Now you

08 Make questions and ask and answer.
Bilden Sie Fragen und befragen Sie sich gegenseitig.

1 💬 What was the weather like yesterday? Was it sunny?
   💬 Yes, it was. (It was lovely.)
   No, it wasn't. (It was awful.)

2 💬 ... you at home last night?
   💬 Yes, I ...
   No, I ...

3 💬 Where ... you last New Year's Eve?
   💬 I was / We were ...
   I can't remember!

4 💬 When was your last holiday?
   💬 It was ...
   I can't remember!

09

28

Ben asks his grandparents about the past. Complete the dialogue.
Then listen and check your answers.
Ben fragt seine Großeltern nach der Vergangenheit. Vervollständigen Sie den Dialog.
Dann hören Sie zu und überprüfen Ihre Lösungen.

was • were • wasn't • weren't

Ben So, what _____ *was* _____ [1] it like when you _____ *were* _____ [2]

my age? I mean, there _____ *was* _____ [3] no internet, right?

Grandpa Yes, that's right. And there _____ *weren't* _____ [4] any computers in my

school. There _____ *was* _____ [5] a telephone in most houses, but

there _____ *weren't* _____ [6] any mobile phones, of course. And

televisions _____ *were* _____ [7] popular, because that was the only way

to watch TV shows or the news. There _____ *were* _____ [8] no tablets.

Ben So, what _____ *were* _____ [9] computers like in the good old days?

Grandma My first computer at work _____ *was* _____ [10] enormous! I remember,

there _____ *was* _____ [11] a big printer in a different room, for printing
letters.

Ben What, no email?

Grandpa No email. Everything _____ *was* _____ [12] very slow. People talk about

the good old days, but they _____ *weren't* _____ [13] so good, you know. For

example, in those days there _____ *weren't* _____ [14] any online meetings.

So, there _____ *were* _____ [15] a lot of business trips and a lot of flights.

Ben And that _____ *wasn't* _____ [16] very good for the planet!

Round up

10

Ask and answer about your past with *was*.
Befragen Sie sich gegenseitig zu Ihrer Vergangenheit mit *was*.

My memories

My first boyfriend / girlfriend
My first teacher
My first school
My first telephone number

My first address
My first car (colour, number)
My first ...

> What was your (*first boyfriend's*) name?

> Who was your (*first teacher*)?

Summary

Was habe ich in dieser Unit gelernt?

COMMUNICATION

Das Wetter

It's a lovely day / morning.
It's nice today.
It was cold yesterday.
It was awful last night.

Erinnerungen

What was it like here in the old days?
It wasn't very nice twelve years ago.
We were both young.
Was it really twelve years ago?

GRAMMAR

Die einfache Vergangenheit: *Was* und *were*

Aussage

I **was** young then.
Sam **was** in Bristol with Bonnie.
You **were** late yesterday.
We **were** at school thirty years ago.
Bonnie and William **were** together.

Verneinung

I **wasn't** very old.
He **wasn't** in L. A.
You **weren't** in the office at nine.
We **weren't** friends then.
They **weren't** married.

Frage

Was Sam a good friend?
Where **was** he last year?
Were you here yesterday?
Were your friends late?
Where **were** Sam and Bonnie?

Antwort

Yes, he **was**. / No, he **wasn't**.
He **was** in America.
Yes, I **was**. / No, I **wasn't**.
Yes, they **were**. / No, they **weren't**.
They **were** on the waterfront.

- I / he / she / it **was**   you / we / they **were**
- wasn't = was not   weren't = were not
- Bei *you* wird immer *were / weren't* verwendet, es heißt also **nicht** ~~you was / wasn't~~.

Ago

He was in Bristol twelve years **ago**.
Er war vor zwölf Jahren in Bristol.

There was only one bar here years **ago**.
Vor Jahren gab es hier nur eine Bar.

- *ago* steht nach der Zeitangabe.

VOCABULARY

Das Wetter		Technik	Die Vergangenheit
sunny	windy	internet	last night
hot	lovely	computer	yesterday
warm	nice	mobile phone	seven years ago
cold	great	tablet	when we were young
wet	awful	printer	in the good old days

Facts & Fun

Übersetzung

29

everyday = alltäglich

conversation = Gespräch, Unterhaltung

surprised = erstaunt, überrascht

quite = ziemlich

personal = persönlich

rude = unhöflich, unverschämt

safe topic = unverfängliches Gesprächsthema

nostalgia = Verklärung

Nice day today?

Many everyday conversations about the weather are very short. Comments like "It's cold today" don't need a full answer. A quick "yes" or "yeah" is enough. The other person is surprised if you say "Well, no, it's quite warm". You talk about the weather when you want to show that you are interested and friendly. That's small talk.

When they make small talk, people from some cultures – the Middle East, China, Southeast Asia, South America and the United States – often ask questions about your age or your job. British people find this too personal or even rude. A Brit often chooses a safe topic – the weather.

Britain's weather changes a lot. You never know what it will be: snow in summer? T-shirts in winter? Brits talk about the weather with everyone they meet. Sometimes they discuss the future ("Will we have a white Christmas?") and sometimes it's nostalgia for the past ("Summers were always better when I was young.").

When do you talk about the weather? How often do you talk about it?

Fun with a crossword

(Lösung auf Seite 157)

				¹W	I	N	D	Y	
	²L	O	V	E	L	Y			
			³R	A	I	N			
	⁴H	O	T						
⁵N	I	G	H	T					
		⁶E	A	R	L	Y			
⁷S	U	M	M	E	R				

1 It's cold and … today.

2 Yesterday was a … sunny day.

3 It was wet, there was a lot of …

4 It was … and sunny on Mallorca.

5 It isn't so warm at …

6 I always get up … in summer.

7 Our winters are cold, but it's always hot in …

Extra Practice

 *Zusätzliche Übungen in der PagePlayer App!*

01   **What's the weather like? Write sentences.**
Wie ist das Wetter? Schreiben Sie Sätze.

cold   hot   wet   windy

1 It's hot.   3 It's windy.
2 It's wet.   4 It's cold.

02   **Put the sentences in the correct order to make a dialogue.**
Bringen Sie die Sätze in die richtige Reihenfolge, sodass sich ein Gespräch ergibt.

Yes, hundreds of balloons. You must go and see them.   Oh, really, was it good?

It was great. There were <u>lots of</u> people.   Yes, why not? I can go on Saturday.

We were at the balloon fiesta yesterday.   And were there many balloons?

🔴 We were at the balloon fiesta yesterday.

🟣 Oh, really, was it good?

🔴 It was great. There were lots of people.

🟣 And were there many balloons?

🔴 Yes, hundreds of balloons. You must go and see them.

🟣 Yes, why not? I can go on Saturday.

03   **Rewrite the sentences. Use *ago*.**
Schreiben Sie die Sätze um. Verwenden Sie *ago*.

1 Sam was in Hong Kong (← 3 years) Sam: I was in Hong Kong three years ago.

2 Bonnie was with William. (← 5 years)

   Bonnie: I was with William five years ago.

3 Sam was in London. (← a week)

   Sam: I was in London a week ago.

4 Sam and Bonnie were new in town. (←12 years)

   Sam: We were in a new town twelve years ago.

04 The police question Max after a robbery in a bank. Complete the sentences.

Die Polizei verhört Max nach einem Bankraub. Vervollständigen Sie die Sätze.

was   wasn't   were   weren't

Detective Where *were* ¹ you yesterday? *Were* ² you in Oxford?

Max No, I *wasn't* ³. I *was* ⁴ at home. I *was* ⁵ twenty miles away in Burford.

Detective And your friends, Eddie and Victor? Where *were* ⁶ they?

Max I don't know. They *weren't* ⁷ with me. And I *was* ⁸ in Burford. It *wasn't* ⁹ me in the bank.

05 Complete the sentences with was, wasn't, were or weren't.

Vervollständigen Sie die Sätze mit *was, wasn't, were* oder *weren't*.

1 The weather was awful yesterday. It *wasn't* very nice.

2 You *were* late this morning. *Was* there a problem with your car?

3 The train *wasn't* five minutes early. It *was* late.

4 What *was* your home like when you *were* a child?

5 There *were* some very cold days last winter.

06 Listen to the dialogue. Match the questions with the correct answers. Then listen again and check your answers.

30

Hören Sie sich den Dialog an. Ordnen Sie die Fragen den passenden Antworten zu.
Hören Sie den Dialog erneut an und überprüfen Ihre Lösungen.

1 What is the woman's dog like?
2 Why was she at her parents' house?
3 What was her holiday like?
4 What was the weather like in Bremen?
5 What was it like in Scotland?

A It was really lovely.
B There weren't any hot days.
C He's very friendly.
D There was a big family party.
E There were two very hot days.

1 C   **2** D   **3** A   **4** E   **5** B

Practise with a partner. Ask and answer the questions.
Üben Sie zu zweit. Befragen Sie sich gegenseitig.

7 We worked together

IN DIESER UNIT LERNEN SIE:

• aus Ihrem Leben zu erzählen

01 🔊 31

Bonnie invites Sam for lunch. Bonnie's children ask him some questions. Listen and repeat.
Bonnie hat Sam zum Mittagessen eingeladen. Bonnies Kinder fragen ihn aus. Hören Sie zu und sprechen Sie nach.

Vena	Where were you born?
Sam	I was <u>born</u> in Santa Fe.
Vena	Where's that?
Sam	It's in New Mexico.

Now you **02**

Practise with a partner. Ask and answer questions.
Üben Sie zu zweit. Befragen Sie sich gegenseitig.

🔴 Where were you born?
🟣 I was born (here) in …
I was born near …

03 Read and listen to the dialogue. Is Sam married?

32

Lesen Sie den Dialog und hören Sie zu. Ist Sam verheiratet?

Answer:
No, Sam is not married.

Vena	Where were you born?
Sam	I was born in Santa Fe.
Vena	Where's that?
Sam	It's in New Mexico. I lived there for 15 years.
Vena	And then?
Sam	Then my family moved to Europe.
Bonnie	Do you have any relatives here now, Sam?
Sam	No, I don't. My parents both died years ago, in 1998. My sister's back in the States.
Bonnie	I'm sorry to hear that. When were you last there?
Sam	Two years ago. We usually meet every year but last year it wasn't possible. We often have video calls of course.
Billy	Were you at school with Mum?
Sam	No, we weren't at school together. We worked together. My first job in the UK was with a newspaper – the Bristol Evening Post. Your mother was a young reporter then. But she was always very smart and now she's the boss!
Bonnie	And Sam's a famous photographer, Billy.
Billy	Are you married? And do you have any children?
Sam	The answer, Billy, is no and no. But I have two nephews and a niece. And of course I'm their favourite uncle.
Vena	My favourite uncle was a banker, but he changed jobs last year. He's a farmer in Ireland now.
Sam	Really? That's interesting.

Quick check

04 Are the sentences true (T) or false (F)? Mark (×) the correct box.

Sind die Sätze richtig (T) oder falsch (F)? Kreuzen Sie an.

EXTRA

Correct the false sentences.

	T	F	
1		×	Sam was born in Europe.
2	×		Sam lived in Santa Fe for 15 years.
3	×		He moved to Europe with his family.
4		×	His parents died in 1989.
5		×	Sam has three children.
6		×	Sam's sister lives in Europe.

05 Language

▶ Page 136

Simple past: regular verbs • Einfache Vergangenheit: reguläre Verben

I work**ed** with your mother.
I live**d** in Santa Fe for 15 years.
We move**d** to England.

They die**d** years ago.
He change**d** jobs last year.

06 Complete the sentences with the past forms of the verbs.

Vervollständigen Sie die Sätze mit den Vergangenheitsformen der Verben.

1 Sam _____ *enjoyed* _____ (enjoy) his lunch with Bonnie's family yesterday.

2 The family _____ *moved* _____ (move) to Europe years ago.

3 The boys _____ *played* _____ (play) football yesterday afternoon.

4 Lisa _____ *wanted* _____ (want) a party on her birthday.

5 The bus _____ *turned* _____ (turn) left into Green Street.

6 The children _____ *helped* _____ (help) in the garden.

7 I _____ *changed* _____ (change) jobs last year.

8 You _____ *phoned* _____ (phone) me very late last night.

Pronunciation

07 Listen and repeat.

33

Hören Sie zu und sprechen Sie nach.

! Achten Sie darauf, dass **-ed** unterschiedlich ausgesprochen wird: als **[t]**, **[d]** oder **[ɪd]**.

[t]	[d]	[ɪd]
looked	answered	contacted
walked	moved	started
watched	remembered	landed
worked	stayed	uploaded

Now you

08 Make four sentences that are true for you from the table.

Bilden Sie vier Sätze aus der Tabelle, die auf Sie zutreffen.

I cooked a meal / dinner / …	last Tuesday.
I emailed some friends / my son / …	yesterday evening.
I worked in a bank / at home / …	when I was young.
I visited my aunt / a museum / …	years ago.
I watched TV / football / …	at the weekend.

 Practise mini dialogues with a partner.
Üben Sie Mini-Dialoge zu zweit.

🔴 I watched TV yesterday evening.
🟣 And I emailed some friends.

Words **09**

34

Listen and repeat.
Hören Sie zu und sprechen Sie nach.

Make questions and answers.
When were you last (*at a party*)?
I was last (*at a party in August 2021*).

1950	nineteen fifty	**2010**	twenty ten
1959	nineteen fifty-nine	**2011**	twenty eleven
2000	two thousand	**2020**	twenty twenty
2009	two thousand and nine	**2024**	twenty twenty-four

10

35

Amy asks her grandmother Charlotte some questions. Listen and complete the information.
Amy stellt ihrer Großmutter Charlotte Fragen. Hören Sie zu und vervollständigen Sie die Angaben.

Charlotte Ramsay

Born: *in 1963   in London*

Moved: *to Bristol when she was 10*

Worked: *in a school as a ballet teacher*

Started: *Charlie's Studio in 2008*

Now: *retired and looks after a little girl called Amy*

Now you **11** **Write three or four complete sentences about your life.**
Schreiben Sie drei oder vier vollständige Sätze über Ihr Leben.

Born: when? where?
Moved: when? where?
Started: school? / work? when?
Worked for: a company? called?

Married? yes / no
Divorced? yes / no
Children? Grandchildren? when born?
Now?

Individual answers

Round up **12** **Talk about your life and add one sentence that is not true.**
Your partner must find the "lie".
Erzählen Sie über Ihr Leben und ergänzen Sie einen Satz, der nicht stimmt.
Ihr Partner/Ihre Partnerin muss die „Lüge" entdecken.

> I was born in Wiesbaden in 1965. My family lived in a castle. I moved to Frankfurt when I was ten. I worked in an office there. I'm not married and I don't have any children. What about you?

> You lived in a castle?! That's not true!

Summary

Was habe ich in dieser Unit gelernt?

COMMUNICATION

Lebensgeschichte

I was born in America. I lived there for five years.
We moved to Stuttgart. I was at school there.

Arbeitsleben

My first job was at a hotel.
Your mother was a young reporter.
She's the boss.
Sam's a famous photographer.
My favourite uncle is a farmer now.

Familie

Are you married?
Do you have any children?
I have two nephews and a niece.
My parents died years ago.

Interesse zeigen

Really? That's interesting.
When were you last at a party?

GRAMMAR

Die einfache Vergangenheit: regelmäßige Verben

I walk**ed** home after the party.
Nach der Party bin ich zu Fuß nach Hause gegangen.
We watch**ed** TV last night.
Gestern Abend haben wir ferngesehen.
Our two sons visit**ed** us last Christmas.
Unsere beiden Söhne haben uns zu Weihnachten besucht.
The family mov**ed** to Scotland two years ago.
Die Familie ist vor zwei Jahren nach Schottland gezogen.

- Bei der einfachen Vergangenheit hängt man bei regelmäßigen Verben *-ed* oder *-d* an das Verb an (walk → walk**ed**, move → mov**ed**).

VOCABULARY

Berufe	Verwandte		Wichtige Ereignisse
dancer	mother	son	I was born
photographer	father	uncle	I lived
reporter	sister	niece	I was at school
shop assistant	brother	nephew	I moved
flight attendant	wife	granddaughter	I worked
teacher	husband	grandson	I changed jobs
farmer	daughter		Now I'm retired
banker			

Übersetzung

36

state = Bundesstaat

border = Grenze

capital (city) = Hauptstadt

colony = Kolonie

Pueblo architecture = Architektur in der Tradition der Pueblo-Ureinwohner

heart = Herz

history = Geschichte

dozen = Dutzend

Spanish-style = auf spanische Art

climate = Klima

Santa Fe, New Mexico

New Mexico is one of the 50 states of America. It is between Texas and Arizona, with the country of Mexico on its southern border. The state capital city is Santa Fe. It's the oldest state capital in America and it's not like any other. In fact, it is called "The City Different".

Why is it different? Perhaps because it feels more Spanish than American. It started as a Spanish colony in 1610 and is famous for its Pueblo architecture. The heart of Santa Fe is still the traditional Plaza. There is colour, history and culture around every corner. The city is a paradise for art lovers. Take a walk down Canyon Road and you can find dozens of art galleries. You can also enjoy Flamenco music and dance and Spanish-style food and drinks.

High in the southern Rocky Mountains, Santa Fe has a wonderful climate with all four seasons and over 300 sunny days per year. This makes it very popular with tourists. English is of course the first language, but over 30 % of the people in Santa Fe speak Spanish.

If you have the chance of a holiday in the USA, why not go to Santa Fe?

Silly jokes

What's the smartest state in America?
(Alabama: has four As and a B!)
In what US state can you find very small drinks?
(Minnesota: Mini-soda!)
What do you call a hippie's wife?
(Mississippi: Mrs. Hippie!)
What US state is round at the ends and high in the middle?
(Ohio!)

Extra Practice

Zusätzliche Übungen in der PagePlayer App!

01   Mark (×) five sentences that are in the past.
Kreuzen Sie die fünf Sätze an, die sich auf die Vergangenheit beziehen.

1		Do you have any relatives here now?
2	×	Were you at school with Mum?
3		Are you married?
4	×	Was it nice there?
5	×	No, we weren't at school together.
6		He's a farmer in Ireland now.
7	×	Then my family moved to England.
8		But I have two nephews and a niece.
9	×	We worked together.

02   Circle eight words for family members.
Kreisen Sie acht Wörter ein, die einen Verwandten oder eine Verwandte bezeichnen.

angel	(brother)	builder	(daughter)
farmer	(grandfather)	(nephew)	teacher
(niece)	passenger	reporter	(sister)
(son)	(uncle)	visitor	woman

03   Complete the sentences.
Vervollständigen Sie die Sätze.

died   lived   moved   remembered   visited   walked   was (2x)

were   worked

Sam _____*was*_____ [1] born in America, and he _____*lived*_____ [2] there for 15 years.

Then his family _____*moved*_____ [3] to Europe. Sam's first job _____*was*_____ [4] in a

newspaper office, where he _____*worked*_____ [5] with Bonnie. He doesn't have any

relatives in England, and his parents _____*died*_____ [6] years ago. Last week

Sam _____*visited*_____ [7] Bristol. He and Bonnie _____*walked*_____ [8] along the

waterfront together.

They _____*remembered*_____ [9] the old days when they _____*were*_____ [10] both young.

04 What did Charlotte do yesterday?
Was hat Charlotte gestern gemacht?

cook   ~~look after~~   phone   play   watch   a friend

a meal   ~~her granddaughter~~   TV   tennis

1 In the morning *she looked after her granddaughter.*

2 Then *she phoned a friend.*

3 In the afternoon *she played tennis.*

4 In the evening *she cooked a meal.*

5 Then *she watched TV.*

05 Listen and circle the correct words. Listen again and check your answers.

37

Hören Sie zu und kreisen Sie die richtigen Wörter ein. Hören Sie erneut zu und überprüfen Sie Ihre Lösungen.

1 Chrissie was last in Zurich   *two* / *three* / *four*   years ago.

2 She was at her   *sister's* / *daughter's* / *best friend's*   wedding.

3 Joss last went to Brussels   *two* / *four* / *six*   months ago.

4 He went to Brazil for his   *mother's* / *best friend's* / *daughter's*   birthday.

06 Write sentences with *favourite*. Add two sentences about yourself.
Schreiben Sie Sätze mit *favourite*. Ergänzen Sie zwei Sätze über sich selbst.

1 David likes autumn. *It's his favourite season.*

2 Sarah likes blue. *It's her favourite color.*

3 Rob likes beer. *It's his favourite drink.*

4 Charlotte likes tennis. *It's her favourite sport.*

5 Richard enjoys a good breakfast. *It's his favourite meal.*

6 Sam's nephews and niece like him. *He's their favourite uncle.*

7 *Individual answers*

8 *Individual answers*

8 Where did you stay?

**IN DIESER UNIT
LERNEN SIE:**

- über Ihren letzten Urlaub zu sprechen

Words   **01**   **Match the sentences with the photographs. Then listen and repeat.**

38   Ordnen Sie die Sätze den Fotos zu. Dann hören Sie zu und sprechen Sie nach.

A We <u>stayed</u> in an <u>apartment</u> near a <u>lake</u>.
B We stayed in a <u>bed and breakfast</u> in the city.
C We stayed at a <u>campsite</u> by the sea.

1 *C*   **2** *A*   **3** *B*

Now you   **02**   **Ask and answer questions about your last holiday.**

Befragen Sie sich gegenseitig zu Ihrem letzten Urlaub.

Useful language
*It was great / lovely / very
nice / OK / very interesting.
We stayed in a hotel.
We stayed at home.
We visited relatives.*

 How was your last holiday?
 It was …
We were in …
We stayed …
What about you?

03 Read and listen to the dialogue. Who is Rufus?

39

Lesen und hören Sie den Dialog. Wer ist Rufus?

Answer:
Rufus is Chris's aunt's dog.

Chris	How was your holiday?
Emma	Great, we were in Wales. It was very nice. What about you?
Chris	We were in Switzerland. That was about a month ago.
Emma	Oh yes, I remember. Where did you stay?
Chris	In a quiet bed and breakfast in the mountains. It was expensive but it was perfect. There were some nice lakes and we walked a lot.
Emma	Hmmm, nice.
Chris	Yes, it was really nice. We loved it, but we can't go there again next year.
Emma	Really? Why not?
Chris	It's difficult to go on holiday with Rufus.
Emma	Who's Rufus?
Chris	My aunt's dog. We look after him now.
Emma	Oh, I see. It isn't very easy to travel with a dog.
Chris	Yes, it's a pity, but Rufus is a great dog and there are a lot of interesting places around here. What about you? Where did you stay? Did you rent an apartment?
Emma	No, we didn't. We hired a camper van for a week.
Chris	What was that like?
Emma	It was OK. The camper van was cheap, but clean. The children played on the beach and watched TV all the time when it rained.
Chris	Ah! Did it rain a lot?
Emma	Yes, it did. Sometimes the rain didn't stop all day!

Quick check

04 Circle the correct answers.

Kreisen Sie die richtigen Antworten ein.

1 Did Chris stay in a hotel?   Yes, he did. / **No, he didn't.**

2 Did he enjoy the holiday?   **Yes, he did.** / No, he didn't.

3 Did Emma stay in a bed and breakfast?   Yes, she did. / **No, she didn't.**

4 Did she stay somewhere cheap?   **Yes, she did.** / No, she didn't.

5 Did the children watch TV?   **Yes, they did.** / No, they didn't.

6 Did it rain a lot in Wales?   **Yes, it did.** / No, it didn't.

05 Language

► Page 137

Simple past: negative and questions • Einfache Vergangenheit: Verneinungen und Fragen

We **didn't stay** in a hotel.   **Did** you **stay** in an apartment?   Yes, we **did.** / No, we **didn't.**

She **didn't rent** a house.   **Did** she **rent** a camper van?   Yes, she **did.** / No, she **didn't.**

Where **did** you **stay**?

06 Complete the sentences with the simple past forms of the verbs.
Vervollständigen Sie die Sätze mit der Vergangenheitsform der Verben.

1 Chris *didn't stay* (not stay) in a hotel, he *stayed* (stay) in a bed and breakfast.

2 They *walked* (walk) in the mountains. They *didn't walk* (not walk) in the city.

3 Chris and his partner *didn't book* (not book) a week, they *booked* (book) two weeks.

4 The children *didn't watch* (not watch) TV shows, they *watched* (watch) films.

5 They *didn't play* (not play) in the park. They *played* (play) on the beach.

6 It *didn't rain* (not rain) in Switzerland, it *rained* (rain) in Wales.

Now you **07**   Say what you did or didn't do last weekend.
Sagen Sie, was Sie letztes Wochenende gemacht oder nicht gemacht haben.

watch TV • cook a meal • visit relatives • call a friend • listen to music • play video games • work • stay at home all day

> I stayed at home all day on Sunday and watched TV. I didn't listen to music.

> I cooked a meal on Saturday and I played video games on Sunday. I didn't visit my relatives.

08   Use the words to make questions.
Benutzen Sie die Wörter, um Fragen zu bilden.

1 Chris / enjoy / his holiday / last year?

   Did Chris enjoy his holiday last year?

2 Emma's children / play / on the beach?

   Did Emma's children play on the beach?

EXTRA

Practise with a partner. Ask and answer the questions.

3 Emma / like / Wales?

   Did Emma like Wales?

4 you / stay / at home / last weekend?

   Did you stay at home last weekend?

5 it / rain / yesterday?

   Did it rain yesterday?

09

40

Kate tells a friend about her holiday. Listen and decide: Which photo did Kate take?
Kate erzählt einem Freund von ihrem Urlaub. Hören Sie zu und entscheiden Sie: Welches Foto hat Kate gemacht?

Listen again and complete the questions.
Hören Sie noch einmal zu und vervollständigen Sie die Fragen.

1 Did you enjoy *your holiday* ?
2 How long *were you away* ?
3 Where did you *stay* ?
4 What was it *like* ?
5 Did you visit *many places* ?
6 What was *the weather* like?

Round up

10

Practise with a partner. Ask and answer questions about your last holiday. Make notes on the answers.
Üben Sie zu zweit. Stellen und beantworten Sie Fragen zu Ihrem letzten Urlaub. Machen Sie sich Notizen zu den Antworten.

> Did you enjoy your holiday?

> Yes, I did. It was very relaxing.

▶ **Useful language:**
like the food?
walk a lot?
watch TV when it rained?

Now work with a new partner. Tell each other about your first partner's last holiday.
Arbeiten Sie mit einem neuen Partner/einer neuen Partnerin. Erzählen Sie einander vom Urlaub Ihres ersten Partners/Ihrer ersten Partnerin.

> Britta enjoyed her holiday. She was away for two weeks. She was in Sweden.

> I love Sweden. It's a very beautiful place.

Summary

Was habe ich in dieser Unit gelernt?

COMMUNICATION

Urlaub

Did you enjoy your holiday? Did it rain?
We were in Switzerland. We loved it.
The children played on the beach.

Unterkunft im Urlaub

Where did you stay?
Did you stay in a bed and breakfast?
What was that like?
We stayed at a campsite by the sea.
We booked a week in a hotel.
We rented a camper van in Scotland.
It was expensive but perfect.

GRAMMAR

Die einfache Vergangenheit: Fragen mit *did*

Frage	*Antwort*
Did you **rent** a car?	Yes, we **did**. / No, we **didn't**.
Haben Sie ein Auto gemietet?	
Did your sister **stay** in a hotel?	Yes, she **did**. / No, she **didn't**.
Hat deine Schwester in einem Hotel übernachtet?	
Where **did** the children **play**?	How long **did** you **stay**?
Wo haben die Kinder gespielt?	*Wie lange sind Sie geblieben?*

- Fragen in der einfachen Vergangenheit bilden wir bei allen Personen mit *did*. Also **nicht** ~~*Rented you a car?*~~
- Die Endung *-ed* entfällt dabei. Also **nicht** ~~*Did you rented a car?*~~

Die einfache Vergangenheit: Verneinung mit *didn't*

It **didn't rain**.   We **didn't like** the hotel.
Es hat nicht geregnet.   *Uns hat das Hotel nicht gefallen.*

- Die Verneinung bilden wir bei allen Personen mit *didn't* (= *did not*).

VOCABULARY

Unterkunft	**Landschaften**	**Wie etwas ist**	
house	mountain	big	clean
apartment	lake	long	nice
hotel	sea	little	lovely
bed and breakfast	beach	old	friendly
camper van	road	new	interesting
campsite	attractions	modern	famous
	sights	quiet	

Facts & Fun

→]
Übersetzung

🔊
41

to **post** = posten
caption = Bildunterschrift
hill = Hügel
definitely = eindeutig
sign = Schild
nearby = nahegelegen
space = Fläche

Tip: Hay-on-Wye = [ˌheɪ ɒn ˈwaɪ]
Conwy Castle = [ˌkɒnwi ˈkɑːsl]

Welcome to Wales

Sometimes people post photos of Welsh beaches on social media with the caption: 'I can't believe I'm in Britain!'. The country of Wales is a part of Britain. It has some beautiful beaches, green hills and a lot of interesting castles and old towns, so it's definitely a good place to visit.

Wales has its own language – called Welsh – and all the signs there are in both English and Welsh. You also hear people speaking the language, especially in North Wales, and it doesn't sound like any other language you know.

If you want to see some highlights while you're on holiday in Wales, why not start with the very nice town of Hay-on-Wye. It's perfect for booklovers because it has more second-hand bookshops than any other town in the world. After that, you can walk in the nearby Brecon Beacons National Park with its green open spaces. Your next stop is Conwy Castle, one of the country's most interesting attractions. It's more than 700 years old! Finish your trip with a beach day in Barmouth, one of the nicest beaches in Wales. And don't forget to enjoy a Welsh cake! It's a small cake that you can eat hot or cold.

Fun with the holiday game

Play this memory game.
The first person says something that they pack in their suitcase for a holiday:
💬 It was holiday time, so I packed sun cream.

The next person says the first thing again and a new thing:
💬 It was holiday time, so I packed sun cream and some T-shirts.

The person after that says the first two things and another new thing:
💬 It was holiday time, so I packed sun cream, some T-shirts and …

Extra Practice

→ *Zusätzliche Übungen in der PagePlayer App!*

01 **Listen to the questions and complete the answers.**
Hören Sie die Fragen und vervollständigen Sie die Antworten.

🔊 42

1   (stay / in a camper van) *We stayed in a camper van.*

2   (rain / every day) *It rained every day.*

3   (watch / TV in the camper van) *We watched TV in the camper van.*

4   (walk / on the beach) *We walked on the beach.*

02 **Write questions with *What … like?* Use the words below.**
Schreiben Sie Fragen mit *What … like?* Verwenden Sie die vorgegebenen Wörter.

concert   food   hotel   beach

1   *What's the hotel like?*   – It's OK. The rooms are very nice.

2   *What was the food like?*   – It was great. I liked all the meals.

3   *What was the beach like?*   – It's nice, and it's good for swimming.

4   *What was the concert like?*   – Very good. I enjoyed all the songs.

03 **Some friends were on holiday in Wales. Make negative sentences.**
Eine Gruppe von Freunden war im Urlaub in Wales. Bilden Sie verneinte Sätze.

1   They rented a house, not a camper van.   *They didn't rent a camper van.*

2   They liked the garden but not the house.   *They didn't like the house.*

3   They stayed ten days not two weeks.   *They didn't stay two weeks.*

4   They booked early, not last minute.   *They didn't book last minute.*

5   They played tennis not football.   *They didn't play football.*

6   They visited castles not museums.   *They didn't visit museums.*

04 Write short answers with *do(n't)*, *does(n't)* or *did(n't)*.
Schreiben Sie Kurzantworten mit *do(n't)*, *does(n't)* oder *did(n't)*.

1 Did you all enjoy your holiday? – *Yes, we did*_____ , thanks. It was great.

2 Does your wife like dancing? – *No, she doesn't*_____ . She can't dance.

3 Do you two live in England? – *Yes, we do*_____ . We live in London.

4 Does your sister work in a restaurant? – *Yes, she does*_____ .

5 Did you like the T-shirt? – *No, I didn't*_____ . It was too big.

6 Do the children walk to school? – *No, they don't.*_____ . I drive them to school.

05 The statements are unclear. Ask for clearer information.
Die Aussagen sind unklar. Fragen Sie nach.

| What ... ? | When ... ? | Where ... ? |

1 We visited London last ... er ... *Sorry? When did you visit?*

2 The children played ... er ... *Sorry? What did the children play?*

3 I started the job in ... er ... *Sorry? When did you start the job?*

4 Years ago Sam lived in ... er ... *Sorry? Where did Sam live?*

06 Write the missing word.
Ergänzen Sie das fehlende Wort.

| aunt | autumn | cinema | eat | expensive | Switzerland |

1	class	school		2	Frankfurt	Germany		3	July	summer
	film	*cinema*			Lausanne	*Switzerland*			October	*autumn*

4	nephew	niece		5	little	big		6	water	drink
	uncle	*aunt*			cheap	*expensive*			food	*eat*

TIPP

Grammatik – mein „Werkzeug" zum Sprechen

Grammatik muss sein, denn sie hilft dabei, sich verständlich auszudrücken. Grammatikregeln sind wie Gebrauchsanleitungen: Mit häufigem Gebrauch automatisieren sie sich. *I am* und *you are* benutzen Sie doch sicher längst ganz automatisch? Also: Regeln zuerst für sich selbst einprägsam formulieren, dann Beispiele hinzufügen und so oft wie möglich wiederholen, trainieren und anwenden – „Practice makes perfect"!

We had a great time

IN DIESER UNIT LERNEN SIE:

- eine Postkarte zu schreiben
- Ferienerlebnisse auszutauschen

Words

01
43

Complete with the simple past forms. Listen and check your answers.
Vervollständigen Sie die Tabelle mit der einfachen Vergangenheitsform der Verben. Hören Sie zu und überprüfen Sie Ihre Lösungen.

came • went • flew • bought • saw • did • took • met • drank

buy	bought	go	went	drink	drank
come	came	meet	met	do	did
fly	flew	see	saw	take	took

Now you

02

Write the past forms of four verbs from exercise 1 in the mind maps. Then say what you did last weekend.
Schreiben Sie vier Verben aus Übung 1 in der Vergangenheitsform in die Mind-Maps. Dann sagen Sie, was Sie letztes Wochenende gemacht haben.

- I **bought** some shoes on Saturday. What did you do, Bianca?
- We **went** shopping in the town centre. What did you do, Max?
- …

03

🔊
44

Read and listen to the two postcards from Chris and Emma from Unit 8.
Where is Chris' dog Rufus?

Lesen und hören Sie die zwei Postkartentexte von Emma und Chris aus Unit 8.
Wo ist Chris' Hund Rufus?

Answer:
Rufus is with Emma.

Dear Emma

We **flew** to Geneva and then **came** here by train. We **had** fondue last night and **drank** Swiss wine. The meal was great, but the waiter wasn't very friendly. We **saw** a beautiful sunset, but the weather's awful now. We **didn't go** on the boat trip on the lake this morning because there was a big storm. I'm so happy Rufus is with you. Thank you again.

Best wishes
Chris

Ms Emma Hirst

5 Queens Road

Bristol

BS8 1QL

England

Hi Chris

I **bought** this postcard at a famous castle. We **did** an interesting tour there two days ago, and **took** some good photographs. We **had** lovely hot weather yesterday. We **went** to the beach and we **had** a great time. It's a beautiful white beach, very clean and quiet. We **met** some people from Switzerland there. Rufus **went** into the sea with the children. They love him! See you next week.

Love
Emma

Chris Baker

11 Hill View

Clifton

Bristol

BS8 7GF

04

Quick check

Circle the correct words.

Kreisen Sie die richtigen Wörter ein.

1 Chris *took a train* / (flew) to Geneva.

2 He *drank beer* / (had fondue.)

3 He (saw a nice sunset) / *went on the boat trip.*

4 Emma (took some) / *didn't take any* good photographs.

5 Her family *didn't have* / (had) a great day.

6 The children (went) / *didn't go* into the sea.

05 Language

▶ Page 137

Simple past: irregular verbs • Einfache Vergangenheit: unregelmäßige Verben

We **flew** to Geneva.   We **didn't fly** to Zurich.   **Did** you **fly** to Zurich?

She **bought** a postcard.   She **didn't buy** a book.   What **did** she **buy**?

06 Complete the sentences with the verbs in the simple past.
Vervollständigen Sie die Sätze mit den Vergangenheitsformen der Verben.

1   We _had_ (have) good food in Switzerland and _drank_ (drink)

    some great wine.

2   Rebecca and Melissa _flew_ (fly) from Berlin and _did_ (do) some

    work on the plane.

3   When I _went_ (go) to Australia last year, I _met_ (meet) some

    people from Frankfurt.

07 Write the questions and answers.
Bilden Sie Fragen und Antworten.

1   your sister / go to New York? – No / Dallas

    Did your sister go to New York? – No, she didn't go to New York.
    She went to Dallas.

2   you / have a big lunch? – No / a quick sandwich _Did you have a big lunch?_
    – No, I had a quick sandwich.

3   your friends / drink wine? – No / beer _Did your friends drink wine?_
    – No, they drank beer.

Now you

08 Practise with a partner. Ask and answer the questions. Make some notes.
Then tell a new partner about your partner.
Üben Sie zu zweit. Stellen und beantworten Sie die Fragen. Machen Sie sich Notizen.
Berichten Sie einem neuen Partner/einer neuen Partnerin.

EXTRA

Make two more questions about last weekend.

1   What / you / have for breakfast today?

2   Where / you / go on your last holiday?

3   You / go shopping last weekend?

Susanne
breakfast:
toast …

09

🔊
45

Complete Will's postcard with the verbs in the simple past. Then listen and check your answers.

Vervollständigen Sie Wills Postkarte mit den Vergangenheitsformen der Verben. Dann hören Sie zu und überprüfen Ihre Lösungen.

Hello from sunny Australia.

The weather's great. We _flew_ [1] (fly) to Sydney for our first week. We _went_ [2] (go) to the famous Opera House and _saw_ [3] (see) an opera there – that was very special. We _did_ [4] (do) a boat trip too.

We _took_ [5] (take) a lot of photos, _drank_ [6] (drink) cold beers and _had_ [7] (have) big steaks on the beach. Last week we _came_ [8] (come) here to Brisbane, a beautiful city. We _bought_ [9] (buy) some nice things for you all. Love Will.

Mr & Mrs Grey

30 Kennel Road

Bower Ashton

Bristol

BS3 2JT

Round up

10

Write a short postcard from a city trip. Use at least four past verb forms.

Schreiben Sie eine kurze Postkarte von einer Städtereise. Verwenden Sie mindestens vier Verben in der Vergangenheitsform.

Dear ...

We're on holiday in England. We came to London yesterday. We went on a boat trip and we saw the London Eye. The weather was nice. London is a great place!

See you next week.
Love from ...

Practise in pairs. Swap postcards. Ask and answer questions about your city trips.

Üben Sie zu zweit. Tauschen Sie Ihre Postkarten. Befragen Sie sich gegenseitig zu Ihren Städtereisen.

What did you see in London?

Who did you meet?

What did you buy?

Where did you have dinner?

Summary

Was habe ich in dieser Unit gelernt?

COMMUNICATION

Eine Postkarte beginnen und beenden

Dear Chris
Hi Emma
See you next week
Best wishes Chris
Love from Emma / Love Emma

Urlaubserlebnisse

We flew to Geneva and then came here by train.
We had fondue and drank Swiss wine.
We did an interesting tour.
We met some people from Switzerland.
We went to the beach and we had a great time.
The meal was great, but the waiter wasn't very friendly.
It was a beautiful white beach, very clean and quiet.

Wetter im Urlaub

The weather is nice / awful now.
There was a big storm.
We had lovely hot weather yesterday.
We saw a beautiful sunset.

GRAMMAR

Die einfache Vergangenheit: unregelmäßige Verben

Chris **had** fondue and **drank** wine.
Chris hat Fondue gegessen und Wein getrunken.

We **saw** a film.
Wir haben einen Film gesehen.

▶ *Eine Liste unregelmäßiger Verben finden Sie auf Seite 137.*

- Es gibt Verben, bei denen man in der einfachen Vergangenheit nicht *-ed* anfügt, sondern die eine unregelmäßige Form haben, z. B. *have → had, drink → drank, see → saw.*

VOCABULARY

Tätigkeiten in der Vergangenheit

ate	met
bought	played
came	saw
cooked	visited
drank	walked
flew	watched
had	went

Gebäude

airport	hotel
bed and breakfast	museum
café	post office
castle	pub
cathedral	restaurant
church	station
cinema	theatre

Facts & Fun

→
Übersetzung

🔊
46

Living history museums

Do you know what a living history museum is? It's a museum where you can walk around, go inside buildings and hear stories about people from the past.

living history museum = Freilichtmuseum

village = Dorf

century = Jahrhundert

to **remember** sth = an etwas erinnern, einer Sache gedenken

Native Americans pl = amerikanische Ureinwohner

stick = Stock, Zweig

to **build, built** = bauen

settler = Siedler/in

hut = Hütte

plant = Pflanze

Tip: Plimoth Patuxet = [ˈplɪməθ] [pəˈtʌksət]

Raupo = [ˈraʊpo]

Maori = [ˈmaʊɹi]

In the USA, living museums are quite popular. A lot of these museums show visitors what life was like for the first Europeans in North America. The Plimoth Patuxet Museum, for example, is an attraction in the town of Plymouth in Virginia. This was where a group of men, women and children from England landed in 1620. You can visit a village and talk to guides in 17th century clothes. The museum remembers that Native Americans lived on this land a long time before the Europeans arrived. You can step inside a *vetu* – a house of sticks and grass – and learn how the Native Americans built it.

In New Zealand, living museums are also popular. One of the biggest and most interesting living history museums there is the Howick Historical Village in Auckland. It shows what early settlers' lives were like. There's a school, a church and there are even *raupo* huts. *Raupo* is a Maori word for a type of plant. These huts were quick and easy for the first settlers in New Zealand to build.

Fun with things from the past

Label the pictures. Then put the inventions in order. Start with the first invention.
Beschriften Sie die Bilder. Dann sortieren Sie sie.
Beginnen Sie mit der ältesten Erfindung.

(Lösung auf Seite 157)

3	2	4	6	1	5

Extra Practice

→ *Zusätzliche Übungen in der PagePlayer App!*

01 Write the English words for these German words. They are all from the postcards on page 75.

Finden Sie die englischen Entsprechungen für die deutschen Wörter. Sie stehen alle auf den Postkarten auf Seite 75.

1 Zug *train*
2 Mahlzeit *meal*
3 Kellner *waiter*
4 freundlich *friendly*
5 Ausflug *trip*
6 froh *happy*

7 berühmt *famous*
8 gestern *yesterday*
9 Strand *beach*
10 sauber *clean*
11 ruhig *quiet*
12 Woche *week*

02 Match the sentences that have a similar meaning.

Ordnen Sie die Sätze denen zu, die eine ähnliche Bedeutung haben.

1 I'm a reporter.
2 It's cheap.
3 It was very wet.
4 I'm very busy.
5 I'm always early.
6 I'm on holiday.
7 I really like this food.
8 It's a popular place.

A I don't have any time.
B I'm never late.
C I'm not at work.
D It doesn't cost very much.
E There are a lot of visitors.
F It rained a lot.
G I work for a newspaper.
H This is my favourite meal.

1 *G*   **2** *D*   **3** *F*   **4** *A*   **5** *B*   **6** *C*   **7** *H*   **8** *E*

03 Complete the answers to the questions about a holiday.

Vervollständigen Sie die Antworten zu Fragen über einen Urlaub.

1 Did Tom fly from <u>Warsaw</u>? – No, *he flew* from Katowice.
2 Did your friends come by car? – No, *they came* by train.
3 Did you all go to the theatre? – No, *we went to* the cinema.
4 Did Helen drink wine? – No, *she drank* water.
5 Did David buy a book? – No, *he bought* a map.
6 Did you meet a friend? – No, *I met* my mother.
7 Did you take a bus? – No, *I took* a taxi.
8 Did Anja eat <u>Spanish</u> food? – No, *she ate* German food.

04

What did Chris and Emma do on holiday? Write a positive sentence after a tick (✓) and a negative sentence after a cross (✗).

Was haben Chris und Emma im Urlaub gemacht? Schreiben Sie entweder einen bejahten (✓) oder einen verneinten (✗) Satz.

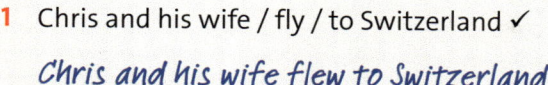

1   Chris and his wife / fly / to Switzerland ✓

Chris and his wife flew to Switzerland.

2   they / go / in their car ✗

They didn't go by car.

3   they / have / fondue ✓

They had fondue.

4   they / drink / German wine ✗

They didn't drink German wine.

5   They / buy / some postcards ✓

They bought some postcards.

6   Emma's family / do / a tour of a castle ✓

Emma's family did a tour of a castle.

7   it / rain / a lot ✗

It didn't rain a lot.

8   the children / play / on the beach ✓

The children played on the beach.

9   The dog / go / into the sea ✗

The dog didn't go into the sea.

05

Write the past forms of the verbs in the crossword. Then you will see a word on the postcards on page 75.

Ergänzen Sie die Vergangenheitsformen der Verben. Senkrecht ergibt sich ein Wort, das auf den Postkarten auf Seite 75 vorkommt.

	¹B	O	O	K	E	D
	²W	E	N	T		
	³C	A	M	E		
⁴B	O	U	G	H	T	
	⁵T	O	O	K		
	⁶V	I	S	I	T	E	D
	⁷F	L	E	W		
⁸T	U	R	N	E	D	
	⁹L	O	O	K	E	D

1   book
2   go
3   come
4   buy
5   take
6   visit
7   fly
8   turn
9   look

Consolidation

10

In dieser Unit wird das Wichtigste aus Units 6 bis 9 wiederholt und vertieft.

AUSSERDEM LERNEN SIE:

• sich im Hotel zu beschweren

01 Read and listen to the <u>reviews</u> of the Grand Hotel. Can you understand the words in red?

47

Lesen und hören Sie Bewertungen über das Grand Hotel. Können Sie die Bedeutung der Wörter in rot erschließen?

× +   − □ ×

'Not great'
The Grand is not a great hotel, but it's OK. The room was clean, but the bathroom wasn't nice at first. The <u>toilet</u> was dirty but they cleaned it for us. The hotel is very near the city centre, and that is very <u>handy</u>.

'Near the <u>sights</u>'
There are shops and good restaurants near the hotel. And it is near the sights. The shower didn't work — the water was cold. But we were happy with the breakfast and the good <u>service</u>. I can recommend it.

'Friendly <u>staff</u>'
We wanted a nice big room, but our room was really small! But it was clean. The staff were very friendly. The next day we <u>moved</u> to a better room. We enjoyed our time at the hotel.

'A lovely time'
We had a lovely time at the Grand. The staff were very friendly and helpful. We had a great room with a <u>view</u> of the park. But the internet <u>connection</u> wasn't very good.

Words **02** Match the words in red in exercise 1 with the German words.

Ordnen Sie die roten Wörter aus Übung 1 den deutschen Begriffen zu.

1 Bad(ezimmer) *bathroom*

2 (Aus-)Blick *view*

3 dreckig *dirty*

4 empfehlen *recommend*

5 klein *small*

6 funktionieren *work*

7 Dusche *shower*

8 Personal *staff*

Quick check **03** Every review mentions a problem. Write a sentence about every problem.

Jede Bewertung erwähnt ein Problem. Schreiben Sie zu jedem Problem einen Satz.

EXTRA

Write a review about a hotel you stayed in.

1 The toilet *was dirty.*

2 *The shower didn't work.*

3 *The room was really small.*

4 *The internet connection wasn't very good.*

04

48

A hotel guest makes a complaint. Read and listen to the dialogue.

Ein Hotelgast beschwert sich. Lesen und hören Sie den Dialog.

Receptionist	Good morning. How can I help you?
Guest	I'm in room 326. The shower doesn't work.
Receptionist	Oh, I'm sorry.
Guest	Can you fix it, please?
Receptionist	Yes, of course. In ten minutes from now. Is that all right?
Guest	Yes, thank you.

Now you **05** Practise with a partner. Act out a complaint dialogue.

Üben Sie zu zweit. Spielen Sie einen Beschwerdedialog nach.

Guest	I'm in room …
	⌐ The *shower / key card / TV / internet* doesn't work.
	⊢ The room is very *cold / small / dirty*.
	⌊ We booked a room with a sea view. But we can't see the sea.
Receptionist	Oh, I'm sorry.
Guest	⌐ Can you fix it, please?
	⌊ Can we have a better room, please?
Receptionist	⌐ Yes, of course. In … minutes from now.
	⌊ Yes, of course. We can give you a new room.
Guest	Thank you.

06

Emily tells a friend about her last holiday. Complete with the verbs in the simple past. Then ask and answer with a partner.

Emily erzählt einer Freundin von ihrem letzten Urlaub. Ergänzen Sie die Verben in der Vergangenheitsform. Befragen Sie sich gegenseitig.

Last month we _____ *went* _____ [1] (go) to Brighton for a holiday. We _____ *stayed* _____ [2] (stay) at a hotel not far from the sea. We really _____ *enjoyed* _____ [3] (enjoy) it. We _____ *had* _____ [4] (have) a great time. The children _____ *played* _____ [5] (play) football on the beach. We _____ *walked* _____ [6] (walk) in the park. And the shops _____ *were* _____ [7] (be) interesting – we _____ *bought* _____ [8] (buy) a lot of new clothes. The weather _____ *was* _____ [9] (be) good – it only _____ *rained* _____ [10] (rain) on one day. We _____ *saw* _____ [11] (see) a James Bond film at the cinema.

▶ to be *in the past tense* = was / were

07

What questions can you ask when someone comes back from a holiday?

Welche Fragen können Sie stellen, wenn jemand aus dem Urlaub kommt?

1 enjoy / last holiday   *Did you enjoy your last holiday?*

2 where / go   *Where did you go?*

3 where / stay   *Where did you stay?*

4 what / do   *What did you do?*

5 see / sights   *Did you see any sights?*

6 rent / car   *Did you rent a car?*

7 what / weather / be like   *What was the weather like?*

8 what / food / be like   *What was the food like?*

08

A woman says how her town is different now. Complete the sentences.

Eine Frau beschreibt, wie sich ihre Stadt verändert hat. Vervollständigen Sie die Sätze.

1 This is a big place now. It *wasn't a big place* in the old days.

2 People have holidays here. *They didn't have holidays here* years ago.

3 There are cars in every street. There *weren't* cars in every street in the old days.

4 Trains stop here now. They *didn't stop here* when I was young.

5 We have nice shops now. We *didn't have nice shops* in the old days.

6 We see a lot of visitors. We *didn't see a lot of visitors* years ago.

7 People take photos. They *didn't take photos* when I was young.

8 This town is famous now. It *wasn't famous* when I was a girl.

EXTRA

Was your town or village different in the old days? Write three sentences about it.

09 Complete the sentences. Listen and check your answers.

🔊 49

Vervollständigen Sie die Sätze. Hören Sie zu und überprüfen Sie Ihre Lösungen.

me • you • him • her • it • us • them

1 **Guest**   I don't have the key to my room. I can't find _____ *it* _____.

Can you help _____ *me* _____, please?

Receptionist Yes, I can give _____ *you* _____ a key. Just a minute, please.

2 **Felix**   Yurek works here. Do you know _____ *him* _____?

Basia   Not really, but his partner is Sonya. I know _____ *her* _____.

3 **Mia**   We met two very nice people from Turkey at our hotel. They were

really interesting. We went with _____ *them* _____ and saw

the sights. And they came with _____ *us* _____ to a restaurant

for dinner.

Ethan   That's cool. Did you enjoy the evening?

Mia   Yes, we all enjoyed _____ *it* _____ very much.

10 Lisa is on holiday. Listen to her call with her mother.
Mark (✗) the correct words on her email.

🔊 50

Hören Sie zu, was Lisa ihrer Mutter in einem Telefonat aus dem Urlaub erzählt.
Kreuzen Sie in der E-Mail die richtigen Wörter an.

💾 ↩ ↻   New Message   — □ ✕

▷   To... [   ]
Send   Subject [   ]

Hi!

How are you?
It's ✗ great   ☐ awful here.
We're in ☐ a hotel   ✗ a holiday apartment
☐ a bed and breakfast.
The people here are ✗ friendly   ☐ not very nice.
I ☐ like   ✗ don't like the food.
The weather is ☐ wet   ☐ cold   ✗ hot.
There are a lot of ☐ beaches   ☐ castles   ✗ lakes.
We ✗ swim   ☐ walk   ☐ watch TV a lot.

Love

Lisa

Review

1. Wie war das Wetter diese Woche? Berichten Sie einem Freund oder einer Freundin.

Monday	Tuesday	Wednesday	Thursday	Friday
28°	22°	16°	18°	8°

I can:

- talk about the weather
- talk about memories of the past
- talk about my life
- write and talk about holidays

2. Sie haben bei einem Foto-Wettbewerb den ersten Preis gewonnen. Schreiben Sie für die Organisatoren eine Kurzbiografie über sich.

I was born ...
I lived in ... for ...years.
Then I moved to ...
My first job was ...
Now I ...

3. Beschreiben Sie für ein Projekt zur Stadtgeschichte, wie Ihre Stadt vor 10, 20 oder 30 Jahren aussah. Erwähnen Sie besonders die Dinge, die sich verändert haben.

4. Verfassen Sie eine Kurzbeschreibung Ihres letzten Urlaubs für Ihre Social-Media-Präsenz. Wo waren Sie, was haben Sie unternommen, wie fanden Sie die Reise?

We went to ...
We stayed at ... for ...
It was ...

▶ Videos

03 Meeting in the bar

03

Enrico is in town for GamesCon, a big games industry convention. He's in the hotel bar, waiting to meet another convention delegate called Steve Newton. Watch the video and answer the questions.

1 Who says these sentences?

	Enrico	Sam
1 There's nobody interesting here.		✗
2 I could never type so fast.	✗	
3 I write interactive storylines.		✗
4 I hope to meet an ex-colleague tonight.	✗	
5 So you're here for GamesCon too?		✗
6 Those games came out before I was born.		✗

2 Why is Sam surprised when Enrico says he's in town for GamesCon?

3 Why is Enrico surprised when Sam says her name?

Talk about video games. Are you interested in them? Do you know anyone who is? Are there big industry conventions near where you live? Do you ever go to one?

04 In the park

04

Sami is walking in the park with her dog Sherlock when her English-speaking friend Melissa runs past her. Watch the video and answer the questions.

1 Sherlock jumps up when he sees Melissa. What does Sami say to the dog? What does she say to Melissa?

2 Circle the correct words.
   A Melissa got back from the UK *a week ago /* *yesterday*
   B Most of the time, she stayed *in a hotel /* *with friends*
   C Sami really *likes* / *doesn't like* London.
   D This year, Sami spent her holiday *at* *home* / *on a walking tour*.
   E The weather *was better /* *worse* for Melissa in England than it was for Sami.

3 At first, Sami hears Melissa say "in the bath". Explain what Melissa really said.

Talk about friends that you meet from time to time, like Sami and Melissa. What do you talk about: pets, holidays, the weather?

Something different

What do you do on your holidays? Do go sightseeing? Do you swim in the sea? Why not do something different next time?

QUEENSTOWN

Queenstown, New Zealand, is the Adventure Capital of the World. There's white water rafting, paragliding, skydiving, mountain biking, horse riding and many other exciting activities. And, of course, bungee jumping from the Karawau Bridge, where AJ Hackett did one of the world's first bungee jumps in 1986.

A RETREAT

Are you always busy? Do you have no time to relax? Too much stress? Maybe a retreat is the answer. When you go on a retreat, you stay at a place in the countryside on your own or in a small group. You try to forget about your daily life and take some time to be quiet and think. On some retreats people also do an activity together like yoga or art.

A LITTLE HELP:

- **something different** etwas anderes
- to **lie** liegen
- **adventure** Abenteuer
- **capital** Hauptstadt
- **paragliding** Gleitschirmfliegen
- **skydiving** Fallschirmspringen
- **horse riding** Reiten
- **exciting** spannend
- **bridge** Brücke
- **retreat** Rückzug
- **countryside** das Land
- **quiet** still

FESTIVALS AROUND THE WORLD

Every month, there are many interesting festivals around the world. On the last Wednesday in August, you can go to *La Tomatina* in Buñol, Spain. Everyone throws tomatoes at each other in the streets and it's great fun for all the family. In January, you can visit the Snow and Ice Festival in Harbin, China. You can see hundreds of beautiful ice sculptures and go dog sledging.

COOKING ON HOLIDAY

Why not learn to cook when you're on holiday? You can do a cooking course for one day and go sightseeing or relax on the other days. First, you usually go to the market to buy food to cook. Your teacher will tell you more about the local food. Then you learn to cook popular dishes from the country. When you get home, you can make these dishes for your friends and family.

A LITTLE HELP:

- to **throw sth** etw werfen
- **ice** Eis
- **sculpture** Skulptur
- to **go dog sledging** Hunde-schlitten fahren
- **local** regional
- **popular** beliebt
- **dish** Gericht

11 How much is it?

IN DIESER UNIT LERNEN SIE:

- Reisepläne zu besprechen
- eine Fahrkarte zu kaufen

Words

01

🔊 51

Match 1–7 with A–G. Listen, check your answers and repeat.

Ordnen Sie 1–7 den passenden Ausdrücken A–G zu. Hören Sie zu, überprüfen Sie Ihre Lösungen und sprechen Sie nach.

A go by bus	**C** go by train
B go by car	**D** go by <u>underground</u>

E walk
F <u>cycle</u>
G fly

1 *E* **2** *F* **3** *B* **4** *C* **5** *A* **6** *G* **7** *D*

Now you

02

Practise in pairs. Ask and answer the questions.

Üben Sie zu zweit. Stellen und beantworten Sie die Fragen.

EXTRA

Ask more questions:

💬 *And what about your friend / partner?*

💬 *She / He usually goes by car, too.*

go shopping • go on holiday • go to work • come to the English class

💬 How do you usually (*go shopping*)?

💬 I (*go by car*). What about you?

03

52

Penny and her friend Freya discuss a day trip to London. Listen and repeat.

Penny und ihre Freundin Freya besprechen einen Tagesausflug nach London. Hören Sie zu und sprechen Sie nach.

Penny	How much is a <u>train ticket</u> to London?
Freya	I'm not sure. It's not cheap.
Penny	Can we go by bus?
Freya	Yes, but that's <mark>slower.</mark> The train is <mark>quicker.</mark>

Now you

04

Ask how you can travel to the different cities.

Fragen Sie, wie man in die verschiedenen Städte reisen kann.

Cambridge • Klosters • Warsaw • Barcelona • Paris • Berlin

EXTRA

Make questions with different towns or cities.

💬 How much is a train ticket to ...?

💬 I'm not sure. *It's not cheap. / It's expensive. / It's not much.*

💬 Can we go by *bus / car / plane?*

💬 *Yes, but that's slower. / Yes, that's quicker.*

05

53

Read and listen to the dialogue. How do Penny and Freya get their train tickets?

Lesen und hören Sie den Dialog. Wie kommen Penny und Freya an ihre Zugtickets?

Answer:
They get their train tickets online.

Penny	A <mark>wet</mark> weekend, again! It's the <mark>wettest</mark> summer I can <u>remember</u>.
Freya	I know. It's awful. Let's go shopping. We can go to London for the day.
Penny	Oh, a <mark>short</mark> trip, that's a nice idea! What about Oxford Street? How much is a train ticket to London?
Freya	I'm not sure. It's not <mark>cheap.</mark>
Penny	Can we go by bus?
Freya	Yes, but that's <mark>slower.</mark> The train is <mark>quicker</mark> and <mark>easier.</mark> Let's <u>check</u> online.
Penny	So how much is a <u>return ticket</u> to London?
Freya	OK ... a <u>day return</u> is £51.50. Oh but a <u>single</u> is £25, so two singles are <mark>cheaper</mark> <u>than</u> a return.
Penny	And do we <u>change trains</u>?
Freya	No, it's a <u>direct train</u>. Look, this is the <mark>best</mark> ticket for us ... £57 and you get a London <u>Travel Card</u> with it, for the underground.
Penny	Let's do that, Freya. I like the underground. It's the <mark>quickest</mark> and <mark>easiest</mark> way to travel in London.
Freya	And this is <u>definitely</u> the <mark>cheapest</mark> ticket. OK so we can book the tickets online and <u>collect</u> them at the station.

At the station

Freya	Come on Penny. We can get our tickets from the <u>machine</u> over there.
Penny	Excuse me, when's the next train to London?
Man	There's a train at ten, it <u>arrives</u> in London at 11:40. Or you can get an <mark>earlier</mark> train, from <u>platform</u> 3, but you only have two minutes ...

Quick check **06** Are the sentences true (T) or false (F)? Mark (×) the correct box.
Sind die Sätze richtig (T) oder falsch (F)? Kreuzen Sie an.

	T	F	
1	×		The train to London is quicker than the bus.
2		×	Two single tickets cost more than a return.
3	×		The best ticket for Penny and Freya costs £57.
4	×		The London Travel Card is for the underground.
5	×		Penny and Freya collect their tickets from a machine.
6		×	The next train <u>leaves</u> at ten.

07 Language
▶ Page 141

Adjectives (1) • Adjektive (1)

slow → slow**er** → slow**est**
quick → quick**er** → quick**est**

The bus is slow**er than** the train.
The quick**est** train is from platform 3.

wet → wet**ter** → wet**test**
big → big**ger** → big**gest**

ear**ly** → earl**ier** → earl**iest**
eas**y** → eas**ier** → eas**iest**

good → **better** → **best**

08 Complete the questions with the correct forms of the adjectives.
Then ask and answer with a partner.
Vervollständigen Sie die Fragen mit den richtigen Formen der Adjektive.
Dann befragen Sie sich gegenseitig.

1 Did you get here _earlier_ (early) or _later_ (late) than the teacher today?

2 What is the _quickest_ (quick) way to the _nearest_ (near) airport?

3 What's the _biggest_ (big) shop in your town?

4 Where is the _best_ (good) restaurant here?

09 Make sentences with _than_.
Bilden Sie Sätze mit _than_.

1 the new hotel / good / the old hotel _The new hotel is better than the old hotel._

2 buses / cheap / trains _Buses are cheaper than trains._

3 cars / quick / buses _Cars are quicker than buses._

4 <u>Spain</u> / hot / England _Spain is hotter than England._

5 Wales / wet / Switzerland _Wales is wetter than Switzerland._

6 Berlin / big / Bonn _Berlin is bigger than Bonn._

Listening **10** Listen to two conversations and a station <u>announcement</u>.
Which is the announcement, 1, 2 or 3?
Hören Sie sich zwei Gespräche und eine Bahnhofsdurchsage an.
Welches ist die Durchsage – 1, 2 oder 3?

1 ☐ The man wants a (single) / *return* ticket to Liverpool. The ticket costs £86 / (£68)

2 ✗ The train to Liverpool now leaves from (platform 3) / *platform 13*.

3 ☐ The 10:55 London train leaves from (platform 1) / *platform 3*.

Listen again. (Circle) the correct words.
Hören Sie noch einmal zu. Kreisen Sie die richtigen Wörter ein.

Now you  **11** Practise in pairs. You are in <u>Italy</u>. Choose a city to visit and find the <u>ticket price</u>.
Then make a dialogue at the station <u>ticket office</u>.
Üben Sie zu zweit. Sie sind in Italien. Suchen Sie sich eine Stadt aus und finden Sie
die Fahrpreise heraus. Formulieren Sie einen Dialog am Fahrkartenschalter.

Passenger	Excuse me, do you speak English?
Assistant	Yes, of course. How can I help you?
Passenger	I'd like a *single / return* ticket to (*Milan*), please.
Assistant	The cheapest *single / return* ticket to (*Milan*) is *21.70 / 43.40* euros.
Passenger	Here you are.
Assistant	Thanks. Here's your ticket.
Passenger	When is the next train?
Assistant	It's at half past four from platform 8.
Passenger	Thank you very much.
Assistant	You're welcome.

Round up **12** Complete the questions with the right words in the right form.
Then ask and answer.
Vervollständigen Sie die Fragen mit den richtigen Wörtern in der richtigen Form.
Danach üben Sie zu zweit.

early • near • good • nice • cheap

1 What's the _____*nicest*_____ building in your town?

2 Who was your _____*best*_____ friend at school?

3 What's your _____*earliest*_____ memory?

4 What's the _____*cheapest*_____ supermarket in your town?

5 What's the _____*nearest*_____ park to your house?

Summary

Was habe ich in dieser Unit gelernt?

COMMUNICATION

Reisen

How much is a ticket to London?
Can we go by bus?
When is the next train?
And do we change trains?

Fahrkarten lösen

A day return is £51.50.
This is the best ticket for us.
We can book the tickets online and pay with a credit card.
We can collect our tickets from the machine.

Vorschläge machen

Let's go shopping.
We can go to London for the day.
That's a nice idea.
What about Oxford Street?

GRAMMAR

Die Steigerung von Adjektiven (1)

It's cold**er** at night.
In der Nacht ist es kälter.

Today is warm**er than** yesterday.
Heute ist es wärmer als gestern.

January is the cold**est** month.
Januar ist der kälteste Monat.

It's the warm**est** day of the week.
Es ist der wärmste Tag der Woche.

- An ein kurzes Adjektiv, z. B. *cold, warm,* fügt man die Endungen *-er* und *-est* an.
- Die Steigerung von längeren Adjektiven folgt in Unit 12.
- In bestimmten Fällen verändert sich die Schreibweise, z. B. *hot → hotter, easy → easier, easiest.*
- Beachten Sie die Sonderformen: *good → better, best.*

▶ *Weitere Einzelheiten finden Sie auf S. 141.*

VOCABULARY

Verkehrsmittel	am Fahrkartenschalter	
by bus	ticket	earlier
by car	single	later
by taxi	return	direct
by train	cheaper	platform
by underground	quicker	
by boat		
walk		
cycle		
drive		
fly		

Underground travel around the world

Übersetzung

55

railway system = Bahnanlage, Schienennetz

rush hour = Hauptverkehrszeit

advice = Rat, Hinweis

women-only carriages = Waggons nur für weibliche Passagiere

cash = Bargeld

The London Underground (usually called the Tube) was the world's first underground railway system when it opened in 1863. The Tube is the fastest and easiest way to travel round the city, but it's very full in the rush hour. The New York City Subway is also over 100 years old. The Subway has 468 stations and they are always open, day and night.

The world's largest underground railway station is in Tokyo, under the city's enormous shopping and entertainment centre. The trains are busy but quiet. The advice to passengers in the metro system's guidebook is: put your mobile in silent mode and do not talk. There are women-only carriages in the rush hour.

But where can you find the best underground system? Perhaps in South Korea. Seoul's subway is the world's longest underground system. It has free internet in all stations and trains. The seats are climate-controlled and automatically warm up in winter. It is clean, easy to use and cheap, but you need cash for the ticket machines — you can't use a credit card.

Do you travel by underground where you live? And when you travel to other countries? What is the best underground system you know?

Fun with a limerick

limerick = ein humorvolles Gedicht in fünf Zeilen

2:02 = den Zug um zwei Uhr zwei (two two)

don't worry = keine Sorge

you don't need to hurry = Sie müssen sich nicht beeilen

to 2:02 = bis zwei Uhr zwei

There was a young lady of Crewe,
Who wanted to catch the 2:02.
Said the train man, 'Don't worry,
You don't need to hurry,
It's a minute or two to 2:02.'

Extra Practice

→ *Zusätzliche Übungen in der PagePlayer App!*

01 **Where did these people travel to and how? Make sentences with** *by*.
Note: the place comes first.
Wohin und wie sind diese Personen gereist? Bilden Sie Sätze mit *by*.
Beachten Sie: Der Ort wird zuerst genannt.

1 *Our teacher went to Paris by train.*

2 My friend *went to Zurich by car.*

3 Flora *went to Glasgow by bus.*

4 Daniel *went to the airport by taxi.*

02 **Complete the conversation. Listen and check your answers.**
Vervollständigen Sie das Gespräch. Hören Sie zu und überprüfen Sie Ihre Lösungen.

56

easier   idea   know   Let's   much   quicker   return   think

Marieke   What about a trip to the shops next week?

Sandy   That's a good _____ *idea* _____ [1]. I need some new clothes.

Marieke   Bus or train? What do you _____ *think* _____ [2]?

Sandy   The bus is cheaper, but the train is _____ *easier* _____ [3].

It's half an hour _____ *quicker* _____ [4] too.

Marieke   _____ *Let's* _____ [5] go by train.

Sandy   OK. How _____ *much* _____ [6] is a ticket?

Marieke   I don't _____ *know* _____ [7], but I can check on the internet. Sometimes

two singles are cheaper than a _____ *return* _____ [8].

03 **You want to take a train to Liverpool. One of these three station announcements has information for you. Listen and complete the sentence.**
Sie wollen mit dem Zug nach Liverpool fahren. Eine dieser drei Durchsagen enthält eine wichtige Information für Sie. Hören Sie zu und vervollständigen Sie den Satz.

57

My train leaves at _____ *10* _____ from platform _____ *2* _____.

04 Make sentences with *cheaper, colder,* etc.
Bilden Sie Sätze mit *cheaper, colder* usw.

1 cheap / train or bus

The bus is cheaper than the train.

2 cold / February or July

February is colder than July.

3 nice / Monday or Friday

Friday is nicer than Monday.

4 big / Poland or Germany

Germany is bigger than Poland.

5 easy / English or French

English is easier than French.

6 early / 6 a.m. or 6 p.m.

6 a.m. is earlier than 6 p.m.

05 Put the words in the correct order.
Bringen Sie die Wörter in die richtige Reihenfolge.

1 from oldest to youngest: grandchildren, grandparents, parents

grandparents, parents, grandchildren

2 from hottest to coldest in your country: autumn, summer, winter

summer, autumn, winter

3 from earliest to latest: afternoon, evening, lunchtime, morning

morning, lunchtime, afternoon, evening

4 from biggest to smallest: building, bus, room, town

town, building, room, bus

5 from longest to shortest: day, hour, minute, month, week, year

year, month, week, day, hour, minute

It looks lovely!

12

**IN DIESER UNIT
LERNEN SIE:**

• Kleidung einzukaufen

01 Bella tries on dresses in a department store. Listen and repeat.

🔊 58

Bella probiert in einem Kaufhaus Kleider an. Hören Sie zu und sprechen Sie nach.

Bella	Excuse me, can I try on this dress?
Assistant	Yes, of course.
	…
Assistant	Is it OK?
Bella	No, it's too big. Do you have a smaller size?
Assistant	Just a minute, please.

Now you

02 Practise with a partner. A is the customer in the shop, B is the assistant.

Üben Sie zu zweit. A ist Kunde/Kundin im Geschäft, B Verkäufer/in.

dress • T-shirt • jacket • pullover

💬 Excuse me, can I try on this (*dress*)?

💬 Yes, of course.

…

Is it OK?

💬 No, it's too *big / small*. Do you have a *smaller / bigger* size?

💬 Just a minute, please.

03

59

Bella and her friend Jaz are in a department store. Listen and read the dialogue. What does Bella try on?

Bella und ihre Freundin Jaz sind in einem Kaufhaus. Hören und lesen Sie den Dialog. Was probiert Bella an?

Bella	Excuse me, can I try on this dress?
Assistant	Yes, of course. The changing room is over there.
	...
	Is it OK?
Bella	No, it's too big. Do you have a smaller size?
Assistant	Just a minute, please. Here you are.
Bella	Great, thanks.
	...
	Jaz, do I look OK in this dress?
Jaz	Yes, very nice. And grey is your colour. It's better than black.
Bella	But is it too short? What do you think?
Jaz	I think it looks lovely, but not with those shoes.
Bella	So I need some new shoes too, but ... oh, I don't know.
Jaz	This isn't the cheapest shop in town.
Bella	No, but it isn't the most expensive. And I think it's the best. The shoe department is on the fourth floor.
Jaz	OK, let's go there.
	...
Bella	Excuse me, can I try on these shoes?
Assistant	Yes, of course.
	...
Bella	Do you have a bigger size?
Assistant	Just a minute, please.
	...
	Here you are.
Bella	Thank you. Ah, these shoes are more comfortable than the others. Yes, I'd like the size 6 shoes, please.
Assistant	Of course.
Bella	OK, now I can buy that dress. And I need a new bag, too.
Jaz	You're worse than me, Bella. Spend, spend, spend ...

Answer: A dress

Quick check ## 04 Circle the correct words.

Was ist richtig? Kreisen Sie ein.

1 Black *is* / *isn't* a good colour for Bella.

2 She *looks* / *doesn't look* better in the grey dress.

3 She *needs* / *doesn't need* new shoes.

4 The shop isn't the *most expensive* / *best* shop in town.

5 The bigger shoes are *more expensive* / *more comfortable*.

6 Bella *spends* / *doesn't spend* more money than Jaz.

05 Language

▶ Page 141

Adjectives (2) • Adjektive (2)

comfortable → **more** comfortable → **most** comfortable
These shoes are **more comfortable than** the others.

expensive → **more** expensive → **most** expensive
It isn't **the most expensive** shop in town.

good → **better** → **best**   bad → **worse** → **worst**

06 Complete the sentences with the correct forms of the adjectives.
Vervollständigen Sie die Sätze mit der richtigen Form der Adjektive.

1 My old shoes are ___more comfortable___ (comfortable) than my new shoes.

2 I have a lot of shoes but my old shoes are the ___most comfortable___ (comfortable).

3 London shops are ___more interesting___ (interesting) than shops in my town.

4 The weather was ___worse___ (bad) yesterday than it is today.

5 That restaurant is the ___worst___ (bad) in town.

6 He bought the ___most expensive___ (expensive) pullover for his partner.

7 That dress looks cheap. Try on a ___more expensive___ (expensive) dress.

8 This bag is the ___most beautiful___ (beautiful) thing in the shop.

EXTRA

Make two more sentences with adjectives.

Now you

07 Make questions. Then ask and answer the questions with your partner.
Bilden Sie Fragen. Danach befragen Sie sich gegenseitig.

1 English / easy / German

___Do you think English is easier than German?___

2 Chinese restaurants / good / French restaurants

___Do you think Chinese restaurants are better than French restaurants?___

3 holiday abroad / interesting / holiday at home

___Do you think a holiday abroad is more interesting than a holiday at home?___

4 trains / comfortable / planes

___Do you think trains are more comfortable than planes?___

5 Tennis / popular / football

___Do you think tennis is more popular than football?___

6 evenings at home / relaxing / evenings in a bar

___Do you think evenings at home are more relaxing than evenings in a bar?___

08 Listen to two conversations in a shop. Which sentence do you hear, A or B?

60

Hören Sie sich zwei Gespräche in einem Geschäft an.
Welchen Satz hören Sie, A oder B?

1.1 A ▢ I'd like a black bag, please.
B ✕ Do you sell black bags?

1.2 A ▢ How much is it?
B ✕ How much does it cost?

2.1 A ✕ You have a pair of red shoes in the window.
B ▢ You have a nice blouse in the window.

2.2 A ▢ Can I try it on, please?
B ✕ Where are the changing rooms?

Now you **09** Practise with a partner. Match the questions and answers.
Then ask and answer the questions.

Üben Sie zu zweit. Ordnen Sie die Fragen den passenden Antworten zu.
Danach befragen Sie sich gegenseitig.

1 Do you need any help?
2 What size are you?
3 How much are they?
4 Can I try them on, please?
5 Here's size 6 – are they better?
6 Do you sell bags?

A No, sorry. We only sell shoes.
B Yes, of course, the changing room's right here.
C No, I'm OK, thanks.
D They're £19.99.
E I'm size 14.
F Yes, they're much better, thank you.

1 C **2** E **3** D **4** B **5** F **6** A

Round up **10** Take notes for a conversation in a shop. Then act out the situation.

Machen Sie sich Notizen für ein Gespräch in einem Geschäft.
Danach spielen Sie die Situation.

long   black   dress
short   white   jacket
little   blue   bag
nice   pink   T-shirt
small   ...

Shoe sizes:	UK	5	6	6.5	7	8
	EU	38	39	40	41	42
Clothes sizes:	UK	10	12	14	16	18
	EU	38	40	42	44	46

Assistant Hello, can I help you?
Customer Yes, please. Do you have (*a little pink jacket*), please?
Assistant What size are you?
Customer I'm size (*14 / 42*).
Assistant Here you are.
Customer How much is it?
Assistant It's (*£45 / €54*).

Summary

Was habe ich in dieser Unit gelernt?

COMMUNICATION

Kleidung kaufen

Can I try on this dress / pullover, please?
Do you have a bigger / smaller size?
Do I look OK in this?
Is it too long / short?
I'd like the size 6 shoes, please.

Vergleiche

It's better than the black dress.
These shoes are more comfortable.
This isn't the cheapest shop in town.
You're worse than me.

GRAMMAR

Die Steigerung von Adjektiven (2)

The dress is **more expensive than** the shoes.
Das Kleid ist teurer als die Schuhe.

This shop is **the most expensive** in town.
Dieses Geschäft ist das teuerste in der Stadt.

- Bei längeren Adjektiven, z. B. *expensive, comfortable,* stellt man bei der Steigerung *more* und *most* voran.

Die Steigerung von *good* und *bad*

The weather today is **better / worse than** yesterday.
Das Wetter ist heute besser / schlechter als gestern.

This is **the best / worst** shop in town.
Dies ist der beste / schlechteste Laden in der Stadt.

- *good* → *better, best*
  bad → *worse, worst*

VOCABULARY

Kleidung
blouse
dress
jacket
pullover
shoes
T-shirt

Kleidung beschreiben
beautiful
big
cheap
comfortable
expensive

long
lovely
nice
short
small

Shinsegae in Busan,
South Korea

Department stores around the world

Übersetzung

🔊 61

food court =
Gastronomiebereich

golf range = Golfplatz

ice-skating rink = Eisbahn

spa = Wellnessbereich

rooftop garden = Dachgarten

coloured-glass and steel

dome = Kuppel aus Buntglas
und Stahl

Art Nouveau = Jugendstil

staircase = Treppenaufgang

probably = wahrscheinlich

Tip: Shinsegae = [ˈʃɪnsegeɪ]

Shinsegae in Busan, South Korea, is officially the world's largest department store.
It is even bigger than Macy's in New York. It has two enormous food courts,
an ice-skating rink, an indoor golf range, a giant spa and a rooftop garden.

Galeries Lafayette has over 200 stores around the world, but its first store in Paris,
France is still the most beautiful. It's famous for its coloured-glass and steel dome
with Art Nouveau staircases and 19 restaurants. And don't miss the store's free
weekly fashion shows.

What about in London? Of course, Harrods in Knightsbridge is the most glamorous
and, at the same time, the largest department store in Europe. Fifteen million people
visit Harrods every year, many of them tourists. They take selfies in its world-famous
Food Hall, but they probably don't buy tea for £5,000 per kilo! This is called "window-
shopping" – you look, but you don't buy. So, when an assistant asks "Can I help you?",
you can smile and say "No thank you, I'm just looking".

Do you shop in big department stores? Do you buy a lot or do you enjoy window-
shopping?

Fun with shop fronts

In welches Geschäft sollte man gehen, um ...

1 eine Zeitung zu kaufen?
2 eine Jacke reinigen zu lassen?
3 einen Schlüssel nachmachen zu lassen?

(Lösung auf Seite 157)

Extra Practice

➡ Zusätzliche Übungen in der PagePlayer App!

01 **What is the perfect gift for these people?**
Welches ist das richtige Geschenk für diese Personen?

birthday cake   book   theatre ticket   football   pullover

1 Our dad likes new clothes. We can *buy him a pullover.*

2 Emma often reads in the evenings. Let's *buy her a book.*

3 My daughter likes sport. We can *buy her a football.*

4 Tom loves musicals. Let's *buy him a theatre ticket.*

5 My grandson is four years old today. We can *buy him a birthday cake.*

02 🔊 62 **Put the sentences in the correct order to start a conversation in a shoe shop. Then listen and check your answers.**
Bringen Sie die Sätze in die richtige Reihenfolge, sodass sich ein Gespräch in einem Schuhgeschäft ergibt. Dann hören Sie zu und überprüfen Ihre Lösungen.

~~Can I help you?~~   Oh, good. Can I try them on, please?   ~~Oh yes, that's better.~~

~~How much are they?~~   Well, I'm not sure. I think they're too small.   They're £60.

OK, I'd like them, please.   We have a bigger size here.

Yes, can I try on these shoes, please?   Yes, of course. … How are they?

💬 *Can I help you?*

💬 *Yes, can I try on these shoes, please?*

💬 *Yes, of course. How are they?*

💬 *Well, I'm not sure. I think they're too small.*

💬 *We have a bigger size here.*

💬 *Oh, good. Can I try them on, please?*

  Oh yes, that's better. How much are they?

💬 *They're £60.*

💬 *OK, I'd like them, please.*

03 Make sentences with *I need* and the *-er*-form of the correct adjectives.
Bilden Sie Sätze mit *I need ...* und der *-er*-Form der passenden Adjektive.

big   cheap   late   long

1   The cashmere scarf is too expensive. *I need a cheaper scarf*.

2   The blue jacket is too short. *I need a longer jacket*.

3   The bag is too small. *I need a bigger bag*.

4   The six o'clock train is too early. *I need a later train*.

04 Complete the sentences.
Vervollständigen Sie die Sätze.

at   for   on   than   with

1   Red isn't a good colour _____ *on* _____ you.

2   The dress is nice but not _____ *with* _____ those shoes.

3   These shoes are more comfortable _____ *than* _____ those.

4   Can we look _____ *for* _____ the jackets?

5   The shoe department is _____ *at* _____ the fourth floor.

05 Match the questions and answers.
Ordnen Sie die Fragen den passenden Antworten zu.

1   Can I help you?
2   Is there a changing room?
3   Do you have a bigger size?
4   Is that the right size for you?
5   Is this dress OK?

A   I'm not sure. Is it too short?
B   No, sorry, we don't.
C   Yes, it is, but not with those shoes.
D   Yes, it's over there.
E   Yes, please. Do you sell jackets?

1 *E*   **2** *D*   **3** *B*   **4** *A*   **5** *C*

06 Complete the sentences with the correct forms of the adjectives.
Vervollständigen Sie die Sätze mit den richtigen Formen der Adjektive.

1   You live in the *nicest* _____ (nice) place in Europe.

2   I think this is the *most interesting* _____ (interesting) programme on TV.

3   Football is the *most popular* _____ (popular) sport here.

4   Sam is the *oldest* _____ (old) person in the office.

5   I think January is the *worst* _____ (bad) time of the year.

I'd like a garden

13

**IN DIESER UNIT
LERNEN SIE:**

- zu sagen, wie und wo Sie wohnen

Words   **01**

63

Match the words with the correct places. Listen, check your answers and repeat.
Ordnen Sie die Wörter den passenden Räumen zu. Hören Sie zu, überprüfen Sie Ihre Lösungen und sprechen Sie nach.

A bathroom

B bedroom

C balcony

D dining room

E kitchen

F living room

G office

H toilet

1 E **2** D **3** F **4** H **5** C **6** B **7** G **8** A

02

64

Jane and her partner Abeeku would like to rent a house. They talk to Satnam the estate agent. Listen and repeat.

Jane und ihr Partner Abeeku möchten ein Haus mieten. Sie sprechen mit dem Makler Satnam. Hören Sie zu und sprechen Sie nach.

Tip: Abeeku = [əˈbiːkuː]
Tip: Satnam = [ˌsætnæm]

Satnam	Where do you live now? In a house or a flat?
Jane	A flat. We only have a little balcony.
Satnam	How many rooms do you have?
Jane	Two bedrooms, a bathroom, a living room and a kitchen.

Now you

03

Ask and answer the questions.

Befragen Sie sich gegenseitig.

- Where do you live? In a house or a flat?
- A (*flat*).
- How many rooms do you have?
- …, …, … and a …

04

65

Read and listen to the complete dialogue. Why does Jane want a bigger house?

Lesen und hören Sie den ganzen Dialog. Warum will Jane ein größeres Haus?

Answer:
She wants a bigger place because her daughter is ten.

Satnam	Jane and Abeeku? Hi, I'm Satnam Singh. Please come in.
Jane	Thank you. This is a beautiful house.
Satnam	Yes, it is. It's a quiet road. There aren't many cars.
Jane	And the garden is very nice. Perfect for Ellie!
Abeeku	Yes, but a big garden is a lot of work and we don't have much free time.
Jane	I'd like a garden. My mother lives in a bungalow with a nice garden.
Satnam	Where do you live now? In a house or a flat?
Jane	A flat. We only have a little balcony.
Satnam	How many rooms do you have?
Jane	Two bedrooms, a bathroom, a living room and a kitchen. Our daughter Ellie has her own room but it's very small. We need a bigger place now because she's six.
Satnam	Well here you have three big bedrooms, a bathroom and a shower room upstairs. There's a toilet downstairs too … and this is the kitchen.
Jane	Wow! It's a lovely big sunny room.
Satnam	There is a dining room too, but you can eat in the kitchen.

Quick check

05

Mark (x) the things that the house has.

Kreuzen Sie an, was das Haus zu bieten hat.

1. ☐ a balcony
2. ☒ kitchen
3. ☒ a shower room
4. ☒ a dining room
5. ☐ four bedrooms
6. ☐ a garden

06 Language
▶ Page 140

a lot of / many / much

+ There are **a lot of** rooms in the house.
  A garden is **a lot of** work.

– There aren't **many / a lot of** cars on this road.
  We don't have **much / a lot of** free time.

? **How many** rooms are there in this flat?   **How much** money do you have?
  Are there **many / a lot of** cars on this road?   Do you have **much / a lot of** work?

07 Circle the correct word(s).
Kreisen Sie das richtige Wort / die richtigen Wörter ein.

1 There aren't *many* / *much* shops near here.

2 We don't have *many* / *much* money at the moment.

3 Were there *much* / *many* students in the class last week?

4 We visited *a lot of* / *much* interesting places on holiday.

5 The boss didn't have *many* / *much* time for us yesterday.

6 There were *a lot of* / *much* new people at my yoga class today.

08 Complete the sentences with *a lot of / many / much*.
Then ask and answer the questions.
Vervollständigen Sie die Sätze mit *a lot of / many / much*.
Dann befragen Sie sich gegenseitig.

1 Do you have _____*a lot of*_____ free time at the weekend?

2 How _____*many*_____ concerts do you go to?

3 Do you buy _____*many*_____ shoes?

4 How _____*much*_____ TV do you watch?

5 Do you do _____*much*_____ sport?

6 Do you read _____*many*_____ books?

 Do you have … free time at the weekend?
(*No, I don't. I work on Saturdays.*) What about you?
…
How … concerts do you go to?
(*I go to a lot of concerts.*) And what about you?

09

66

Complete the dialogue with the correct words. Then listen and check your answers.
Vervollständigen Sie den Dialog mit den richtigen Wörtern.
Danach hören Sie zu und überprüfen Sie Ihre Lösungen.

flat • toilet • bathroom • house • shower

Ellie	Granny, we moved to a new house yesterday!
Betty	I know. You're a lucky girl.
Ellie	Why?
Betty	Because you have a big _____*house*_____ ¹ now.
Ellie	Where did you live when you were young?
Betty	We lived in a _____*flat*_____ ² so we didn't have a garden.
Ellie	Did you have your own room?
Betty	No, I shared a room with my two sisters. The bedroom was always cold.
Ellie	Why?
Betty	We didn't have central heating then.
Ellie	No heating? Did you have a _____*bathroom*_____ ³ in your flat?
Betty	Of course we did, but we didn't have a _____*shower*_____ ⁴ in it like you.
Ellie	Did you have a _____*toilet*_____ ⁵?
Betty	Of course we did! I'm not that old, Ellie!

Round up ## 10

Where did you live as a child? What did or didn't you have? Write a text, then read it to your group. Ask and answer questions.
Wo haben Sie als Kind gewohnt? Was hatten Sie, was nicht? Schreiben Sie einen Text und lesen Sie ihn der Gruppe vor. Dann befragen Sie sich gegenseitig.

I lived in a house / a flat / a bungalow.

We had a toilet downstairs when I was young.

My brothers and I had our own rooms.

We didn't have a big garden.

We didn't have a dining room so we had all our meals in the kitchen.

Did you have a computer?

Did you have a balcony?

Did you have a bath?

Summary

Was habe ich in dieser Unit gelernt?

COMMUNICATION   **eine Wohnung beschreiben**

Do you live in a house or a flat?
How many rooms do you have?
My mum lives in a bungalow.
We have two bedrooms.
We don't have a garden.
We need a bigger house.

Komplimente

This is a beautiful house.
The garden is very big.
The living room is lovely.

GRAMMAR   *a lot of, many* und *much*

+	There are **a lot of** rooms upstairs.	*viele Zimmer*
	The house costs **a lot of** money	*viel Geld*
–	There aren't **many / a lot of** shops here.	*nicht viele Geschäfte*
	We don't have **much / a lot of** money.	*nicht viel Geld*
?	**How many** rooms are there in the flat?	*Wie viele Zimmer gibt es in der Wohnung?*
	Are there **many / a lot of** rooms in the flat?	*Gibt es viele Zimmer in der Wohnung?*
	How much money do we have?	*Wieviel Geld haben wir?*
	Do we need **much / a lot of** money?	*Brauchen wir viel Geld?*

- *A lot of* kann man in bejahten und verneinten Sätzen sowie Fragen benutzen.
- *Many* und *much* benutzt man hauptsächlich in verneinten Sätzen und in Fragen.
- *Many* benutzt man mit Pluralformen, z. B. *rooms, shops; much* mit Wörtern wie *money, food* usw.

VOCABULARY

Wo man wohnt
house
flat / apartment
bungalow

Zimmer
living room
dining room
kitchen
bathroom
toilet
bedroom
balcony

Stockwerke
downstairs
upstairs
on the ground / first / second floor

Facts & Fun

→ Feeling at home

Übersetzung

🔊 67

When people in the UK and the US talk about their homes, they're usually more interested in how many bedrooms and bathrooms it has, rather than how big it is. Some people in these countries build their own homes (especially if they live in the countryside), but this isn't as important as it often is in Germany.

especially = besonders, insbesondere

in the countryside = auf dem Land

one-storey = einstöckig

condominium, condo = Eigentumswohnung

terrace, terraced house = Reihenhaus

connected = verbunden

Let's look at three types of houses that you can find in English-speaking countries. First, we have a bungalow. The word *bungalow* comes from the Hindi word *bangla*, which means *Bengali*, and Britons in India used it to describe the low one-storey houses that Bengalis often built. Then there is a condominium (condo for short). This type of home is popular in the USA and condos are parts of one bigger building that different people or families own. Finally, we have terraced houses, which you often see in big cities in the UK. In a terrace you have four or more houses that are connected to each other. Sometimes all of the houses on one street are a terrace.

Fun with your perfect home

**Think about your perfect home. Talk about it in small groups.
Answer the questions – and don't hold back!**
Überlegen Sie, wie Sie gerne wohnen würden. Reden Sie in kleinen Gruppen darüber. Beantworten Sie die Fragen – und hauen Sie ruhig auf den Putz!

1 Is it a house or a flat?

2 What rooms are in it?

3 Does it have a garden or a balcony or both?

4 Is it in the town centre or in the countryside?

5 What is special? Do you have a big garden, a swimming pool, …?

Extra Practice

→ *Zusätzliche Übungen in der PagePlayer App!*

01 **What are the names of the rooms? Write the words on the plan.**
Wie heißen die Zimmer? Schreiben Sie die Wörter auf den Plan.

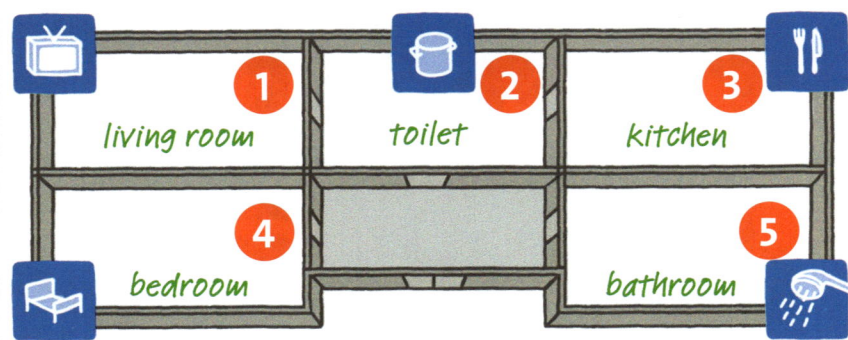

1 *living room*
2 *toilet*
3 *kitchen*
4 *bedroom*
5 *bathroom*

02 **Put the words into the correct group.**
Ordnen Sie die Wörter den richtigen Rubriken zu.

bathroom   breakfast   castle   church   dinner   hot   nephew

kitchen   lunch   house   parent   sister   sunny   toilet   wet

Rooms: *bathroom, kitchen, toilet*

Buildings: *castle, church, house*

Meals: *breakfast, dinner, lunch*

Relatives: *nephew, parent, sister*

Weather: *hot, sunny, wet*

03 **Make sentences with *a lot of*.**
Bilden Sie Sätze mit *a lot of*.

	~~buys~~		~~dresses.~~
He	watches		games.
She	drink	a lot of	red wine.
They	plays		places.
	visit		series.

1   Rosa loves clothes. *She buys a lot of dresses.*

2   Dascha likes TV. *She watches a lot of series.*

3   Alex plays games on the computer. *He plays a lot of games.*

4   My friends often go on bus tours. *They visit a lot of places.*

Tip: Alicja = [əˈlɪsjə]   5   Matthew and Alicja like wine. *They drink a lot of red wine.*

04 Write the negative forms of the sentences with *many* or *much*.
Schreiben Sie verneinte Sätze mit *many* oder *much*.

1 There are only five guests in the hotel.

There aren't many guests at the hotel.

2 There are only two oranges and some <u>tuna fish</u> in the kitchen.

There isn't much food in the kitchen.

3 There are only two rooms in the flat.

There aren't many rooms in the flat.

4 There's only fifty pence in my jacket.

There isn't much money in my jacket.

05 Complete the questions with *How many* or *How much*.
Ergänzen Sie die Fragen mit *How many* oder *How much*.

1 *How much* money do you have in your <u>pockets</u>?

2 *How many* cars are there in the car park?

3 *How many* bedrooms are there in this house?

4 *How much* free time do you have at the weekend?

06 Read the property ads and answer the questions.
Lesen Sie die Immobilienanzeigen und beantworten Sie die Fragen.

Victoria Road £695 / month 2 bedroom flat near town centre
Park Road £895 / month 3 bedroom modern house with nice garden
West Street £825 / month 2 bedroom house with garage
Albert Road £780 / month 2 bedroom first floor flat
Castle Street £795 / month 3 bedroom bungalow
Church Street £650 / month 1 bedroom flat with balcony on third floor
King Street £1495 / month lovely 4 bedroom house on three floors

Where can you find …

1 a flat with only one bedroom? *Church Street*

2 a house with a garden? *Park Road*

3 a flat on the first floor? *Albert Road*

4 a house with four bedrooms? *King Street*

5 a flat near to the city centre? *Victoria Road*

14 I hate gardening

IN DIESER UNIT LERNEN SIE:

- über Freizeitaktivitäten zu sprechen
- über Ihre Vorlieben und Abneigungen zu sprechen

Words

01

68

Match the words with the free time activities. Listen and check your answers.

Ordnen Sie die Wörter den Freizeitaktivitäten zu. Hören Sie zu und überprüfen Sie Ihre Lösungen.

1	2	3	4
5	6	7	8

A	cooking	**C**	dancing	**E**	gardening	**G**	baking
B	cycling	**D**	fishing	**F**	reading	**H**	running

1 F   **2** A   **3** D   **4** H   **5** B   **6** E   **7** C   **8** G

02

69

Tina meets her new neighbour Brad on the stairs. Listen and repeat.

Tina lernt im Treppenhaus ihren neuen Nachbarn Brad kennen. Hören Sie zu und sprechen Sie nach.

Brad	I hate gardening, so I like living in a flat now!
Tina	Same here.
Brad	What do you like doing in your free time?
Tina	I don't have much free time, but I love cycling.

Now you **03** Practise with a partner. Ask and answer questions about your free time activities.

Üben Sie zu zweit. Befragen Sie sich gegenseitig zu Ihren Freizeitaktivitäten.

baking • cooking • cycling • dancing • fishing • gardening • reading • running

💬 What do you like doing in your free time?

💬 I *like / love (cooking)*. And you?

04 🔊 Read and listen to the dialogue. What do Tina and Brad do at the end of the conversation?

70

Lesen Sie den Dialog und hören Sie zu. Was machen Tina und Brad am Ende des Gespräches?

Answer:
They look at Tina's bike.

Tip: Ahmad = [əˈmɑːd]

Tina	Hi. Are you our new neighbour?
Brad	That's right. I'm Brad.
Tina	My name's Tina. Good to meet you.
Brad	You too.
Tina	So, do you like the flat?
Brad	Yes, we love it. We lived in a house before. I hate gardening, so I like living in a flat now!
Tina	Same here.
Brad	What do you like doing in your free time?
Tina	I don't have much free time, but I love cycling.
Brad	Really? Me too.
Tina	I usually go with my partner, Ahmad.
Brad	I live with my partner Lucy, but she doesn't like cycling with me. She likes running and swimming.
Tina	I really hate running!
Brad	Me too. You can go a lot faster on a bike! Can I ask you a question? I need a new bike …
Tina	I have a really good bike, but it was expensive. Come and have a look. …

Quick check **05** Who likes what? Complete the sentences with the correct names.

Wer mag was? Vervollständigen Sie die Sätze mit den richtigen Namen.

1 ____Brad____ and ____Tina____ don't like gardening.

2 Both ____Tina____ and ____Brad____ love cycling.

3 ____Lucy____ doesn't like cycling with ____Brad____.

4 ____Lucy____ likes swimming and running.

5 ____Tina____ and ____Brad____ don't like running.

06 Language

▶ Page 137

like / love / hate + -ing

What do you **like** do**ing** in your free time?

I **love** cycl**ing**.   I **hate** cook**ing**.

07 Complete the sentences with the *-ing* form of the correct verb.

Vervollständigen Sie die Sätze mit der *-ing*-Form des passenden Verbs.

cycle • dance • do • go • help • listen to

1 Tina has an expensive bike because she loves _____ *cycling* _____.

2 My husband doesn't like _____ *doing* _____ yoga.

3 My mother loved _____ *dancing* _____ the tango when she was younger.

4 Do you like _____ *listening to* _____ music in the evening?

5 The dog hates _____ *going* _____ for walks in the rain.

6 Brad doesn't like _____ *helping* _____ his dad in the garden.

08 Ahmad has a coffee with Lucy. Listen and decide: Which diagram is for Ahmad and which is for Lucy?

🔊 71

Ahmad trinkt mit Lucy einen Kaffee. Hören Sie zu und entscheiden Sie: Welche Grafik passt zu Ahmad, welche zu Lucy?

- cooking   + cycling

1 *Lucy*

+ making cakes   + dancing

Lucy doesn't like cooking.

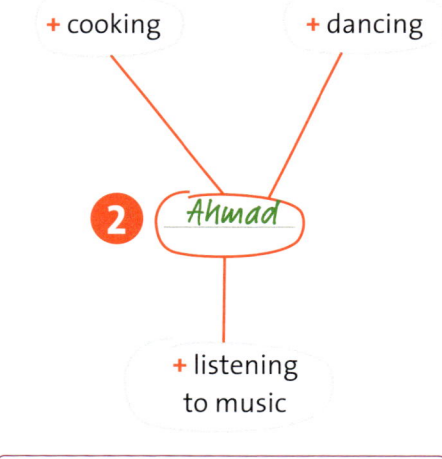

+ cooking   + dancing

2 *Ahmad*

+ listening to music

Ahmad and Lucy both like dancing.

Now you **09**

How do you <u>relax</u> in the evenings or at the weekend?
Ask and answer questions with a partner.
Wie entspannen Sie sich abends oder am Wochenende?
Befragen Sie sich gegenseitig.

reading • listening to music • <u>chatting to friends</u> • watching TV •
having a cup of tea • drinking a glass of wine • playing computer games

💬 Do you like (*reading*) in the evenings?

💬 ⌐ No, I don't. I don't find it relaxing. What about you?
  └ Yes, I do. I love it. I find it very relaxing. What about you?

EXTRA

Tell another student about your partner's free time activities.

> My partner likes going for a walk with her dog in the evenings. She finds it relaxing.

Round up **10**

You meet someone on holiday. What do you want to know about him / her?
Write questions. Then ask and answer with a partner.
Im Urlaub lernen Sie jemanden kennen. Was möchten Sie über ihn / sie erfahren?
Schreiben Sie Fragen auf. Danach befragen Sie sich gegenseitig.

Do you come here every year?	Yes, we always come in August.
How many children do you have?	Three. Two boys and a girl. What about you?
Do you do any sport?	No, but I like watching it on TV.
Do you like cooking?	No, I don't. But my partner loves it. He's a very good cook.

Summary

Was habe ich in dieser Unit gelernt?

COMMUNICATION   **Freizeitaktivitäten**

What do you like doing in your free time?

I love dancing.

I like cooking.

I hate gardening.

I find reading relaxing.

I don't have much free time.

Do you do any sport?   Yes, I do. I love it. / No, I don't. I hate it.

Does your partner cycle?   Yes, she does. / No, she doesn't.

GRAMMAR   *Like / love / hate + Verb mit -ing*

My partner **loves** bak**ing** cakes.
Meine Partnerin backt gerne Kuchen.

Brad **hates** garden**ing**.
Brad hasst Gartenarbeit.

Do you **like** cook**ing**?
Kochen Sie gerne?

VOCABULARY   **Freizeitaktivitäten**

baking (cakes)	going to parties
cooking	listening to music
cycling	meeting friends
dancing	playing computer games
eating out	reading (books)
fishing	shopping
gardening	singing
going on holidays	swimming
going to concerts / the cinema / the theatre	walking

Dancing around the world

Übersetzung

72

square = öffentlicher Platz
similar = ähnlich
dance move = Tanzschritt
to take place = stattfinden
adult = Erwachsene/r
to become = werden
success = Erfolg
alone = allein
back = Rücken
straight = gerade

In China, over 100 million people enjoy square dancing. It's called this because people dance in big squares or parks in China's cities. Most of the dancers are older or retired women. They come together to dance in the morning or the evening. All of the dancers do the same or similar dance moves at the same time while the music plays, so it's interesting to watch.

Tango is a mix of Spanish flamenco dancing, African dance and other dance styles too, but the Argentinians put all of these styles together. There are many tango cafés on the streets of big Argentinian cities. Everyone can come together to dance and have fun.

In Ireland, Irish dance is a very popular hobby for both children and adults. It became famous around the world after the success of the musical *Riverdance* in the 1990s. Irish dancers dance alone or in a line. They all do the same moves at the same time. The dancers keep their backs very straight and move their feet very quickly.

Fun with a quiz

1 **What season starts in September?**
☐ spring   ☐ summer   ✗ autumn

2 **Where can you see a famous balloon fiesta?**
✗ in Bristol   ☐ in Liverpool   ☐ in London

3 **Where is Australia's most famous opera house?**
☐ in Brisbane   ☐ in Melbourne   ✗ in Sydney

4 **What is the name of a famous shopping street in London?**
☐ Cambridge Street   ☐ Dover Street   ✗ Oxford Street

(Lösung auf Seite 157)

Extra Practice

01 What do these people like doing? Make sentences with the *-ing* form.
Then write what you like doing in your free time.
Was machen diese Personen gerne? Bilden Sie Sätze mit der *-ing*-Form.
Danach schreiben Sie auf, was Sie gerne in Ihrer Freizeit tun.

→ *Zusätzliche Übungen in der PagePlayer App!*

cycle   eat out   garden   shop   swim   walk

1 He likes gardening.
2 They like walking.
3 They like shopping.

4 He likes swimming.
5 They like eating out.
6 She likes cycling.

And you? Individual answers

02 Complete the sentences with the correct form of the verb.
Vervollständigen Sie die Sätze mit der richtigen Form des Verbs.

1 David *likes cooking* (cook) the Sunday lunch.

2 My friends often *eat out* (eat out) at expensive restaurants.

3 My husband hates *dancing* (dance), so he never comes with me.

4 When did you *come* (come) back from your holiday?

5 I hate *filling in* (fill in) forms!

6 I don't like *working* (work) at weekends.

7 We *moved into* (move into) our new house two weeks ago.

8 My wife *gets up* (get up) early every morning.

9 Can I *try on* (try on) these shoes please?

10 We love *going* (go) to hot and sunny places on holiday.

03 Match the questions with the correct answers.

Ordnen Sie die Fragen den passenden Antworten zu.

1	Are you our new neighbour?	A	I sometimes play tennis.
2	When did you move in?	B	Two weeks ago.
3	Do you like the house?	C	Yes, I'm Richard.
4	What do you do in your free time?	D	Yes, it's nicer than our old flat.
5	Does your wife play tennis?	E	Yes, she does.
6	How about a game of tennis tomorrow?	F	Great idea!

1 *C* **2** *B* **3** *D* **4** *A* **5** *E* **6** *F*

04 Complete the explanations with the correct words.

Vervollständigen Sie die Worterklärungen mit den passenden Wörtern.

1 Your neighbour lives in the next house or _____*next door*_____ .

2 A kitchen is a _____*place*_____ where you cook.

3 When you cycle, you go by _____*bike*_____ .

4 Your aunt is your mother's or father's _____*sister*_____ .

5 In a changing room you can try on new _____*clothes*_____ .

6 A bungalow is a house on one _____*level*_____ .

05 Circle the word that doesn't belong in the group.

Kreisen Sie das Wort ein, das nicht dazugehört.

1 bike, car, train, (wife)

2 dress, jacket, (shower,) T-shirt

3 (awful,) lovely, perfect, super

4 dancing, swimming, (working)

5 left, (of course,) right, straight on

6 dinners, friends, neighbours, (staff)

7 both, double, (single,) two

8 enjoy, (hate,) like, love

TIPP

Gibt es Wörter, die Sie sich einfach nicht merken können? Vielleicht klappt es ja so: Schreiben Sie die Wörter einzeln und gut lesbar auf Kärtchen, auf der Vorderseite auf Englisch, auf der Rückseite in Ihrer Muttersprache. Sie können auch einen Beispielsatz oder eine Beispielfrage mit dem Wort notieren. Lesen Sie die einzelnen Kärtchen immer wieder. Legen Sie beiseite, was Sie sich gemerkt haben. Doch werfen Sie es nicht weg, sondern wiederholen Sie es in größeren Abständen.

Consolidation

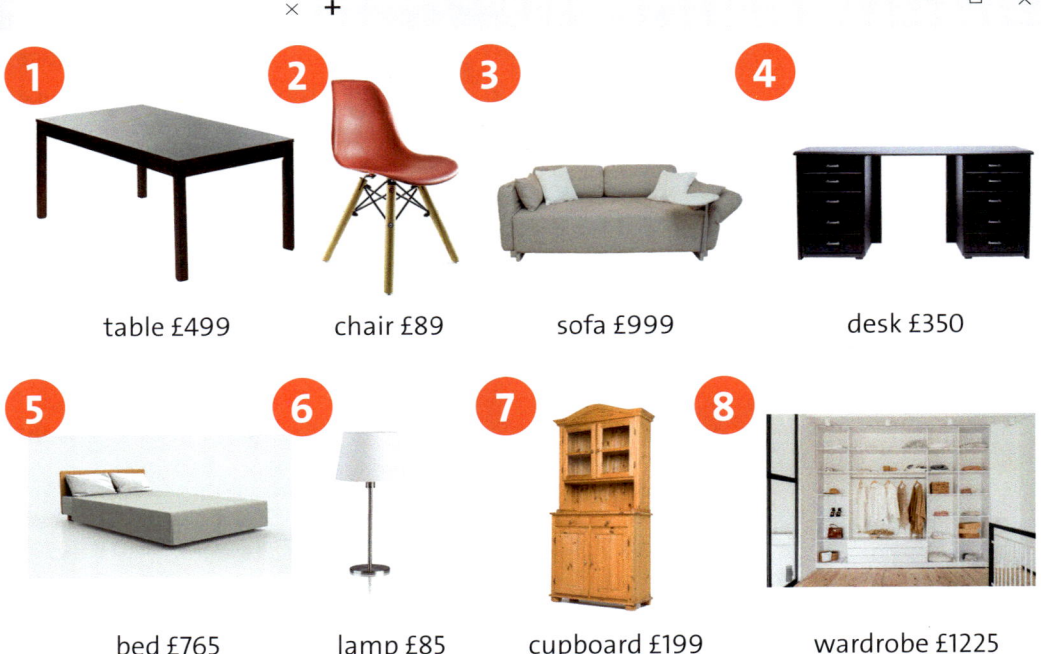

In dieser Unit wird das Wichtigste aus Units 11 bis 14 wiederholt und vertieft.

AUSSERDEM LERNEN SIE:

- Wortschatz im Bereich Möbel

1 table £499

2 chair £89

3 sofa £999

4 desk £350

5 bed £765

6 lamp £85

7 cupboard £199

8 wardrobe £1225

01 Match the sentences with the furniture.
Ordnen Sie die Sätze den Möbeln zu.

A It's the cheapest thing. *6*

C It costs more than seven hundred pounds. *5*

B It's the most expensive thing on this website. *8*

D It costs a hundred and ninety-nine pounds. *7*

02 Compare the prices in exercise 1.
Vergleichen Sie die Preise in Übung 1.

1 table – chair *The table is more expensive than the chair.*

2 desk – bed *The desk is cheaper than the bed.*

3 wardrobe – sofa *The wardrobe is more expensive than the sofa.*

4 lamp – cupboard *The lamp is cheaper than the cupboard.*

03

73

Read and listen to the dialogue. Joel and Simon look at a furniture website. Who wants a new sofa, Joel or Simon?
Lesen und hören Sie den Dialog. Joel und Simon sehen sich eine Möbel-Website an. Wer möchte ein neues Sofa haben, Joel oder Simon?

Simon	This website is interesting. These chairs look nice.
Joel	Mm, they're OK.
Simon	We need some chairs for the dining room. And a table.
Joel	Yes, of course. We didn't have a dining room in the flat.
Simon	And a table lamp for the living room.
Joel	We need carpets too. The old carpets aren't the right size.
Simon	OK, new carpets, too. At least we have the sofa.
Joel	Yes, but we bought this sofa years ago.
Simon	Only four or five years ago.
Joel	We bought it at least six years ago.
Simon	But it's fine. It's so comfortable. I like it.
Joel	I don't like the colour. I want nice new things, Simon. Let's get a new sofa.
Simon	All this furniture is so expensive.
Joel	Yes, but this house is much bigger than our flat. We need a new wardrobe for the bedroom.
Simon	Can we order these things online?
Joel	Yes, of course we can, but let's go to the store where we can look at the furniture. We have no plans this weekend.
Simon	I hate shopping but … OK. There's a big store only five miles from here.

Answer:
Joel wants a new sofa.

Quick check ## 04 **Mark (x) the four things Simon wants to buy.**
Kreuzen Sie die vier Dinge an, die Simon kaufen will.

☐ a bath	☐ a cupboard	✕ carpets
✕ some chairs	✕ a table	☐ a desk
☐ a sofa	✕ a table lamp	☐ a wardrobe
☐ a bed	☐ a TV	

05

Match the descriptions with words from the dialogue.
Ordnen Sie den Beschreibungen Wörter aus dem Dialog zu.

1 a big shop *store*

2 chairs, tables, beds, etc. *furniture*

3 a room where you eat your meals *dining room*

4 a big cupboard for clothes *wardrobe*

5 a shop online with photos of things and prices *website*

06   Circle the correct words.
Kreisen Sie die richtigen Wörter ein.

1   How   *many* / *much* does it cost?

2   You can't dance. You're *worse* / *worst* than me.

3   The pullover is *more* / *most* expensive than the T-shirt.

4   There are *a lot of* / *much* rooms upstairs.

5   I hate   *work* / *working* on Saturdays.

6   We moved in a month *ago* / *away*.

07   Write sentences with *many* and *much*.
Schreiben Sie Sätze mit *many* und *much*.

books • money • passengers • wine

1   *She doesn't have much money.*

2   *There aren't*   *many passengers on the bus.*

3   *There aren't many books on the shelf.*

4   *He doesn't have much wine.*

08

**Joel and Simon are at a café. Complete the sentences.
Then listen and check your answers.**

74

Joel und Simon sind in einem Café. Vervollständigen Sie die Sätze.
Dann hören Sie zu und überprüfen Sie Ihre Lösungen.

better (2x) • best • worse • worst

Simon	Where's the <u>waitress</u>? She's very slow. The service here is the
	_____**worst**_____ ¹ in Bristol.
Joel	But the coffee here is very good. It's
	_____**better**_____ ² than at Lisa's Coffee Shop. This is the
	_____**best**_____ ³ place for coffee.
Simon	There's _____**better**_____ ⁴ service at Lisa's, but we can't
	go there now.
Joel	Yes. Look at the rain. Yesterday was bad, but this is
	_____**worse**_____ ⁵ .

EXTRA

Do you know a good café in your town?

09

**Alek wants to rent a holiday house from Mrs Wilkins.
He calls her with some questions. Listen and write the words you hear.**

75

Alek will bei Mrs Wilkins ein Ferienhaus mieten. Er ruft sie an, um einige Fragen zu klären. Hören Sie zu und schreiben Sie die Wörter auf, die Sie hören.

1 address:
   16 Green Street
2 How far from the sea?
   five minutes' walk
3 Number of bedrooms:
   two

4 Dining room?
   yes
5 Size of garden:
   not big
6 Rent per week:
   850 pounds a week

10

Complete the translations with two words in every sentence.
Vervollständigen Sie die Übersetzungen mit jeweils zwei Wörtern pro Satz.

1 Es waren nicht viele Autos auf dem Parkplatz.

There weren't _____**many cars**_____ in the car park.

2 Ein Zug ist schneller als ein Auto.

A train is _____**faster than**_____ a car.

3 Ich kaufe gerne Möbel für die Wohnung.

I like _____**to buy furniture**_____ for the flat.

4 Die Jacke sieht sehr schön aus.

The jacket _____**looks**_____ nice.

Review

I usually go to work by car. What about you?

1. Look at this list. Tell a partner how you usually go to each place.

- your work
- a friend's home
- a relative's home
- on holiday
- your local shopping centre

2. Your friend wants to buy a blue jacket. The friend's size is medium and he doesn't want to pay more than fifty euros. Look at these three jackets. Tell your friend which jacket is right for him and why.

I can ...

- talk about travel plans
- buy clothes
- talk about my home
- talk about free time activities
- talk about likes and dislikes
- use words for furniture

3. You see this advertisement for a home to buy. Tell a partner about the home in English.

Schönes Haus in Zentrumsnähe

Dieses Haus ist perfekt für Familien. Es hat im Erdgeschoss ein Wohnzimmer, ein Esszimmer, eine Küche und eine Toilette. Im ersten Stock gibt es drei Schlafzimmer, ein Badezimmer und einen Balkon. Das Haus hat einen Vorgarten und einen Garten an der Rückseite. Es liegt in einer ruhigen Straße nahe dem Stadtzentrum.

4. You meet a new neighbour. You want to find out if you like the same free time activities. Think of:
   - one activity you love
   - two activities you like
   - two activities you don't like
   - one activity you hate
   Your new neighbour is another student. Find out if you like the same activities. Find an activity you can do together.

What do you like doing in your free time?

Videos

05 The dinner party

05

Tomasina and her German partner Moritz are going to a dinner party at his boss's house. Watch the video and answer the questions.

Mark (✗) the correct answer.

1 What does Moritz hate doing?
  A ☐ going to office parties **B** ☐ being late for dinner
  C ✗ wearing a tie

2 Why does Tomasina try on a different dress?
  A ✗ Because she thinks the orange dress is too short.
  B ☐ Because Moritz thinks the orange dress is too short .
  C ☐ Because she has nothing to wear.

3 Tomasina doesn't know when the party begins because
  A ☐ she lost the invitation. **B** ☐ the invitation wasn't in English.
  C ✗ Moritz has the invitation.

4 Moritz didn't know that a "fancy dress party" means
  A ☐ you mustn't be late. **B** ✗ you must come in a costume.
  C ☐ you must wear chic clothes .

Do you like dressing up and going out? Talk about costume parties. Do you like them? What do you know about "Dinner for One"?

06 City apartment or town house?

06

Hetty and Toni are talking about what they can do with Hetty's parents' apartment. Watch the video and answer the questions.

Mark (✗) the sentences. Are they true (T) or false (F)?
Correct the sentences that are not true.

		T	F
1	Toni doesn't understand why Hetty is sad.		✗
2	Hetty lived in the apartment when she was a child.	✗	
3	Hetty's not happy with her mother's care home.		✗
4	The apartment has too many rooms and too much furniture.	✗	
5	Hetty loves cooking in her mother's old kitchen.		✗
6	The women agree to change the apartment into an Airbnb.	✗	

What does Hetty say about her mother's care home? Talk about the older members of your family or older people that you know. Where do they live? Where would you like to live when you're older?

Unusual homes

Not everyone lives in a normal house or flat. Some people live in the strangest homes: old train stations, lighthouses, windmills, castles, old churches, old schools, and even tree houses.

TINY HOUSES

A 'tiny house' must have a floor area of no more than 37 square metres. But it must have everything you usually find in a house, like a bathroom and a kitchen. Many people build and live in tiny houses because they want to live in a simple way and help the environment. 'Tiny houses' are also cheap and easy to build.

A HOME IN THE AIR

Joanne Ussery lives next to a lake in Benoit, Mississippi. Her home is a Boeing 727. It flew for 25 years, and then the airline didn't want it. Joanne paid $2,000 for the plane, $4,000 to transport it and $24,000 to renovate it. It has a living room, a kitchen, three bedrooms, a bathroom and four toilets with 'No smoking' signs. Her grandsons think she's the coolest grandmother in the world.

A LITTLE HELP:

- **unusual** ungewöhnlich
- **lighthouse** Leuchtturm
- **windmill** Windmühle
- **even** sogar
- **tree house** Baumhaus
- **tiny** winzig
- **floor area** Bodenfläche
- **square metre** Quadratmeter
- to **build sth** etw bauen
- **environment** Umwelt
- to **renovate sth** etw renovieren
- **smoking** Rauchen

ON THE WATER

What about a houseboat? This couple lives on a houseboat. A boat like this can have a living room, a kitchen, a bedroom and a bathroom with a shower.
This type of boat is called a 'narrowboat' because, as you can see, it's very narrow.
But, it's fine for tidy people.

UNDERGROUND

Coober Pedy is a small town in South Australia and a centre of opal-mining. It is often very hot in the summer – sometimes more than 40°C – and many people live in underground caves where they can stay cool. There are underground shops, museums and churches too.

A LITTLE HELP:

- **type** Art
- **narrow** eng, schmal
- **tidy** ordentlich, aufgeräumt
- **underground** unterirdisch
- **mining** Bergbau
- **cave** Höhle

Grammar Overview

Grammar terminology · Grammatische Begriffe

Englisch	Deutsch	Beispiel / Erklärung
adjective	Adjektiv, Eigenschaftswort	*good, cold, hungry, modern* usw.
adverb of frequency	Häufigkeitsadverb	I **never** watch sport. • We **often** meet at the pub.
comparative	Komparativ, erste Steigerungsform	*cheaper, longer, more modern, more expensive*
comparison	Steigerung, Vergleich	**older** than me, a **more comfortable** seat, the **nicest** place in England, the **most expensive** sweater in the shop
consonant	Konsonant, Mitlaut	*b, c, d, f, g, h, j, k* usw.
countable	zählbar	Zählbare Substantive können im Singular oder im Plural stehen, z. B. *book/books, car/cars*. Nicht zählbare Substantive haben keine Pluralform, z. B. *meat, water, cash*.
demonstrative	hinweisender Begleiter	*this, that, these, those*
ing-form	ing-Form	I like **watching** tennis. • I hate **doing** this job.
negative	negativ, Verneinung	mit *not* oder *n't: I'm* **not** *sure*. • He is**n't** here.
noun	Substantiv, Nomen, Hauptwort	*cake, man, words, milk, seat, computers* usw.
object	Objekt, Satzergänzung	Have **a nice flight**. • I do **yoga**. • We visited **him**.
past	Vergangenheit, Imperfekt, Präteritum	I **enjoyed** the concert. • We **took** some photos.
personal pronoun	Personalpronomen, persönliches Fürwort	*I, me, you, he, him, she, her, it, we, us, they, them*
phrase of time	Zeitangabe	We get up **at half past seven**. • My evening class is **on Thursday**.
plural	Plural, Mehrzahl	Substantive im Plural sind z. B. *names, girls, classes, churches*.
preposition	Präposition, Verhältniswort	*in, on, at, for, from* usw.
present	Präsens, Gegenwart	It **is** four o'clock. • **Are** you OK? • I **like** cheesecake.
question	Frage	*Where is the bus stop? • Do you like this sweater?*
question word	Fragewort	*what, where, when, how* usw.
sentence	Satz	z. B. eine Aussage, eine Frage oder ein Befehl
short answer	Kurzantwort	Is he Irish? – **Yes, he is**. • Can you sing? – **No, I can't**.

short form	Kurzform	In Kurzformen wird ein Teil eines Wortes durch einen Apostroph (') ersetzt, z. B. **I'm** = I am, **you're** = you are, **isn't** = is not, **don't** = do not, **didn't** = did not.
sibilant	Zischlaut	*class, zero, shop, cheers, just*
simple past	einfache Vergangenheit	*I **enjoyed** the concert. • We **took** some photos.*
simple present	einfache Gegenwart	*We **live** in Germany. • She **takes** the train. • I **know**.*
singular	Singular, Einzahl	Substantive im Singular sind z. B. *name, girl, class, church.*
statement	Aussage	Ein Satz, der etwas behauptet: *The city is big. • It costs £15.*
subject	Subjekt, Satzgegenstand	***Tessa** plays tennis. • Our **gate** is number 12. • **I** was at home.*
superlative	Superlativ, höchste Steigerungsform	*cleanest, greatest, most relaxing, most comfortable*
third person singular	dritte Person Singular	Nach einem Ausdruck wie *Mary, the man, a beer, he, she, it* steht ein Verb in der dritten Person Singular, z. B. *Mary work**s** here.*
third person plural	dritte Person Plural	z. B. *they, the trains, your books*
verb	Verb, Zeitwort, Tätigkeitswort	*take, eats, do, visits, see, go, took, went*
vowel	Vokal, Selbstlaut	*a, e, i, o, u*

Grammar overview · Grammatikübersicht

CONTENTS · INHALT

01 The present of *have* · Die Gegenwart von *have*

**A STATEMENT ·
AUSSAGE**

I **have** an idea.

You **have** a new car.

The children **have** passports.

- Mit *I, you, we* und *they* verwendet man *have*.

Darius **has** two jobs.   Olivia **has** a job interview.

- In der dritten Person Singular (z. B. *Darius,* Olivia, *he, she, it*) verwendet man *has*.

We **don't have** time.

Does Setare **have** children? – **Yes, she does**.

- Die Verneinung und Fragen bildet man wie bei anderen Verben.

**B HAVE = EAT/DRINK ·
HAVE = „ESSEN/
TRINKEN"**

What time do you **have lunch?**   Jane **has coffee** for breakfast.
Um wie viel Uhr essen Sie zu Mittag?   *Zum Frühstück trinkt Jane Kaffee.*

- „Essen" und „trinken" wird manchmal durch *have* ausgedrückt, z. B. *have a meal, have a sandwich, have an orange juice.*

02 The simple present · Die einfache Gegenwart

A FORMS · FORMEN

Aussage	Verneinung	Frage	Kurzantwort
I / You / We / They **work**.	I **don't work**.	**Do** you **work?**	Yes, I **do**. / No, I **don't**.
He / She **works**.	He **doesn't work**.	**Does** he **work?**	Yes, he **does**. / No, he **doesn't**.

**B STATEMENT ·
AUSSAGE**

I **know** the way.   We **like** old films.

You **read** a lot of books.   The children **play** games.

- Mit *I, you, we* und *they* verwendet man in der einfachen Gegenwart die Grund-
form des Verbs, z. B. *know, read.*

Darius **knows** the way.   Rosa **misses** her daughter.

The sweater **looks** nice.   My sister **likes** old films.

- In der dritten Person Singular (z. B. *Darius, the sweater, Rosa, my sister, he, she, it*) fügt man ein *s* an das Verb (*know → knows, like → likes, look → looks*). Nach einem Zischlaut (z. B. *ss*) wird *es* angehängt (*miss → misses*).
- Die einfache Gegenwart verwendet man, um einen Zustand auszudrücken, z. B. was man denkt oder fühlt (*I know, she likes*). Man benutzt sie auch, um Handlungen zu beschreiben, die sich (regelmäßig) wiederholen (*you read a lot of books*).

C   NEGATIVE •   VERNEINUNG

Langform	Kurzform
I **do not know** the way.	I **don't know** the way.
Setare **does not play** computer games.	Setare **doesn't play** computer games.

- Bei *I, you, we* und *they* bilden wir die Verneinung mit *do not*. In der dritten Person Singular (mit *he, she* und *it*) bilden wir die Verneinung mit *does not*. *Do not* wird zu *don't* und *does not* zu *doesn't* verkürzt.

D   QUESTION • FRAGE

Do you **know** the way? – Yes, of course.

Where **do** the children **play**? – In the garden.

Does your son **visit** you? – Yes, sometimes.

What time **does** Darius **start** work? – Seven o'clock.

- In einer Frage mit *I, you, we* und *they* wird *do* verwendet. Also **nicht** ~~Know you the way?~~ oder ~~Where play the children?~~
- In der dritten Person Singular wird *does* verwendet. Also **nicht** ~~Visits your son you?~~ oder ~~What time starts Darius work?~~

E   SHORT ANSWER •   KURZANTWORT

Do you walk to the office? – **Yes, I do**. / **No, I don't**. I take the bus.

Do Emma and Sam work here? – **Yes, they do**. / **No, they don't**.

Does Setare make the sandwiches? – **Yes, she does**. / **No, she doesn't**.

Does the flight cost much? – **Yes, it does**. It's £500. / **No, it doesn't**. Not very much.

03 The position of phrases of time · Die Stellung der Zeitangaben

Helen starts work	**at half past eight**.
We go to yoga class	**every Wednesday evening**.
Do you have a sandwich	**at lunchtime?**
I can work	**Saturdays**.

- Ein Ausdruck der Zeit, z. B. *at half past eight,* steht am Ende des Satzes und **nicht** mitten im Satz.

04 The position of adverbs of frequency · Die Stellung der Häufigkeitsadverbien

We **always** go to the pub for lunch.	I **sometimes** look after my grandson.
The children **usually** watch TV.	Richard **never** drinks beer.
Our daughter **often** visits us.	

- Die Häufigkeitsadverbien (*always, usually* usw.) stehen normalerweise mitten im Satz, vor dem Verb in der einfachen Gegenwart (*go, watch* usw.). Also **nicht** ~~We go always to the pub for lunch~~.

I'm **always** busy.

The bus is **often** late.

- Die Häufigkeitsadverbien stehen aber **hinter** einer Form von *be,* z. B. *am always, is often*.

Sometimes I look after my grandson.

I look after my grandson **sometimes**.

- *Sometimes* kann auch am Anfang oder am Ende stehen.

05 The past of *be* • Die Vergangenheit von *be*

A FORMS • FORMEN

I **was**	*ich war*
you **were**	*Sie waren / du warst / ihr wart*
we **were**	*wir waren*
he / she / it **was**	*er war / sie war / es war*
they **were**	*sie waren*

B STATEMENT • AUSSAGE

I **was** at home yesterday.

The film **was** very good.

- *Was* verwendet man nach *I* und in der dritten Person Singular (nach *he, she, it*).

You **were** late yesterday morning.

We **were** in London last weekend.

All the sights **were** interesting.

- *Were* verwendet man nach *you*. Also **nicht** ~~you was~~. *Were* steht auch nach *we* und in der dritten Person Plural, z.B nach *they, all the sights*.

C NEGATIVE • VERNEINUNG

Langform	**Kurzform**
It **was not** sunny yesterday.	It **wasn't** sunny yesterday.
You **were not** here on Monday.	You **weren't** here on Monday.

- Die Verneinung bilden wir mit *not*. *Was not* wird zu *wasn't* und *were not* zu *weren't* verkürzt.

D QUESTION AND ANSWER • FRAGE UND ANTWORT

Where **was** Bonnie yesterday? – At the swimming pool.

Was the film good? – It was OK.

Was Sam in the office? – **Yes, she was**. / **No, she wasn't**. She was at home.

When **were** your friends here? – Last week.

Were you two in the Park Hotel. – **Yes, we were**. / **No, we weren't**.

Were you at the fiesta? – **Yes, I was**. / **No, I wasn't**. Not this year.

- In einer Frage steht *was* oder *were* vor dem Subjekt: *Was Sam …?, Were you …?*
- Beachten Sie, dass Fragen mit ***Were** you …?* an eine einzelne Person mit der Kurzantwort *Yes, I was. / No, I **wasn't*** beantwortet werden.

06 The simple past • Die einfache Vergangenheit

A FORMS • FORMEN

Regelmäßige Verben:	I work**ed** at home yesterday. *Ich habe gestern zu Hause gearbeitet.*
Unregelmäßige Verben:	We **took** some photos. *Wir haben einige Fotos gemacht.*
Verneinung:	I **didn't eat** sandwiches. *Ich habe keine Sandwiches gegessen.*
Frage:	**Did** you **enjoy** the concert? *Hat das Konzert Spaß gemacht?*
Kurzantwort:	Yes, I **did**. / No, I **didn't**.

B REGULAR VERBS • REGELMÄSSIGE VERBEN

We **played** tennis yesterday.

We all **liked** the tour.

The bus **stopped** at the traffic lights.

Jane **started** work early.

- Um die einfache Vergangenheit zu bilden, fügt man *ed* an das Verb (*play → played*). Die Form ist in allen Personen gleich (*we played, you played, he played* usw).
- Wenn das Verb aber auf *e* endet, wird nur *d* angehängt (*like**d***).
- Wenn ein einsilbiges Verb auf einen einzelnen Vokal und einen einzelnen Konsonanten endet, wird der Konsonant vor *ed* verdoppelt: *stop → sto**pp**ed*. Das gilt aber **nicht** bei zwei Vokalen (*look → looked*), bei zwei Konsonanten (*turn → turned*) oder bei *y* oder w (*stay → stayed*).
- Die Endung *ed* spricht man meistens wie *t* oder *d* aus und **nicht** als eine zusätzliche Silbe. Nur wenn das Verb selbst auf *t* oder *d* endet, spricht man *ed* als Silbe aus: *start**ed***.

C IRREGULAR VERBS • UNREGELMÄSSIGE VERBEN

We all **had** a great time at the weekend.

I **went** to the cinema yesterday.

Tessa **bought** a cashmere sweater.

- Einige Verben haben in der Vergangenheit eine unregelmäßige Form. Das sind meistens häufig vorkommende Verben, die man einfach lernen muss. Die Form ist in allen Personen gleich (*we had, you had, he had* usw.).

buy → bought	*find → found*	*know → knew*	*sing → sang*
come → came	*fly → flew*	*leave → left*	*spend → spent*
cost → cost	*get → got*	*make → made*	*take → took*
do → did	*give → gave*	*meet → met*	*teach → taught*
drink → drank	*go → went*	*say → said*	*tell → told*
drive → drove	*have → had*	*see → saw*	*think → thought*
eat → ate	*keep → kept*	*sell → sold*	*understand → understood*

**D NEGATIVE •
VERNEINUNG**

Langform

I **did not eat** breakfast.

Daniel **did not see** his friends.

Kurzform

I **didn't eat** breakfast.

Daniel **didn't see** his friends.

- Die Verneinung bildet man in allen Personen mit *did not* (Kurzform: *didn't*).

**E QUESTION AND
ANSWER • FRAGE
UND ANTWORT**

Where **did** you **buy** that T-shirt? – At the shop in Station Road.

How much **did** it **cost**? – Only £6.

Did you **visit** the museum? – **Yes, we did. / No, we didn't**. There was no time.

Did your husband **go** with you? – **Yes, he did. / No, he didn't**.

- In einer Frage wird *did* verwendet. Also **nicht** ~~Visited you the museum?~~ oder ~~Went your husband with you?~~
- Kurzantworten bildet man mit *did* oder *didn't*.

07 *Like/love/hate* + ing-form • *Like/love/hate* + ing-Form

Do you **like** listen**ing** to music?
Hören Sie gern Musik?

I **love** visit**ing** nice places.
Ich besuche gerne schöne Orte.

My wife **hates** fly**ing**.
Meine Frau fliegt sehr ungern.

- Folgt nach *like, love* und *hate* ein weiteres Verb, so steht es in der ing-Form (z. B *listening*).

08   The irregular plural of nouns • Der unregelmäßige Plural der Substantive

Singular	Plural
one person	five **people**
a man	three **men**
a woman	some **women**
the child	the **children**

- Um den Plural (die Mehrzahl) von Substantiven zu bilden, hängt man normalerweise *s* oder *es* an (*room – rooms, class – classes*).
- Nur wenige Wörter haben eine unregelmäßige Pluralform. Zu diesen Formen zählen *people, men, women* und *children*.

09   Personal pronouns • Personalpronomen

Subjektform	Objektform
I'm in this photo.	Can you see **me?** *mich*
You were in town yesterday.	I saw **you** with Lisa. *dich*
Where's Felix? Is **he** with you?	I can't find **him**. *ihn*
Where's Sonya? Is **she** with you?	I can't find **her**. *sie*
Our hotel is the Bristol. **It**'s very good.	I like **it**. *es*
We have some luggage.	Can you give **us** some help? *uns*
The children? **They**'re in the park.	Basia took **them**. *sie*

- *He/him* ist männlich und *she/her* ist weiblich.
- *They/them* ist die Mehrzahl von *he/him*, von *she/her* und auch von *it*.
- Diese Pronomen haben nur **eine** Objektform: *me* = mich/mir; *him* = ihn/ihm; *them* = sie/ihnen.

10 *Some* and *any* • *Some* und *any*

A BASIC USE •
ALLGEMEINER
GEBRAUCH

Aussagesätze

Richard has **some** photos.

Richard hat ein paar Fotos.

I need **some** milk.

Ich brauche (etwas) Milch.

Verneinte Sätze

I can't see **any** taxis.

Ich sehe keine Taxis.

We don't have **any** water.

Wir haben kein Wasser.

Fragen

Are there **any** buses on a Sunday?

Fahren sonntags Busse?

Do you have **any** information?

Haben Sie Informationen?

- *Some* benutzt man in positiven Aussagen, *any* in verneinten Aussagen und in Fragen.
- *Some* und *any* verwendet man mit Substantiven im Plural (*some photos*) oder mit nicht zählbaren Substantiven (*some milk*).
- Nicht zählbare Substantive haben keine Pluralform. Auch *information* ist im Englischen nicht zählbar. Es heißt also *some/any information*, **nicht** ~~an information~~ und **nicht** ~~any informations~~.

**B OFFERS AND
REQUESTS** •
ANGEBOTE UND
BITTEN

Angebot

Would you like **some** coffee?
Möchten Sie (etwas) Kaffee?

Bitte

Can I have **some** chips, please?
Kann ich bitte (ein paar) Pommes frites haben?

- In Angeboten und Bitten benutzt man eher *some* als *any*.

11 A lot of, many and much • A lot of, many und much

Positive Aussagen	Martin reads **a lot of** books.	*viele Bücher*
	We eat **a lot of** fish.	*viel Fisch*
Verneinte Aussagen	There aren't **many** hotels / **a lot of** hotels here.	*nicht viele Hotels*
	I don't drink **much** wine / **a lot of** wine.	*nicht viel Wein*
Fragen	**How many** emails are there?	*wie viele E-Mails*
	Do you speak **many** languages / **a lot of** languages?	*viele Sprachen*
	How much time do we have?	*wie viel Zeit*
	Did Betty spend **much** money / **a lot of** money?	*viel Geld*

- *A lot of* kann man in positiven Aussagen, in verneinten Aussagen und in Fragen verwenden.
- *Many* und *much* verwendet man hauptsächlich in verneinten Aussagen und in Fragen. Man kann sie mit *how* kombinieren. *How many* heißt „wie viele" und *how much* heißt „wie viel".
- *Many* verwendet man mit Substantiven im Plural, z. B. *hotels, emails*. *Much* verwendet man mit nicht zählbaren Substantiven, z. B. *wine, time*.

12 Demonstratives: *this, that, these and those* • Hinweisende Begleiter: *this, that, these* und *those*

	in der Nähe	weiter entfernt
Singular	**This** coffee is good.	Can you see **that** boat?
Plural	Can I try on **these** shoes?	**Those** mountains are 20 miles from here.

- *This* und *these* beziehen sich auf etwas in der Nähe, *that* und *those* auf etwas, das weiter entfernt ist.
- *These days* = „heutzutage". *In those days* = „damals".

13 The comparison of adjectives · Die Steigerung von Adjektiven

A ONE-SYLLABLE ADJECTIVES AND TWO-SYLLABLE ADJECTIVES WITH Y ·
EINSILBIGE ADJEKTIVE UND ZWEISILBIGE ADJEKTIVE AUF Y

Komparativ

I need a **smaller** size.

The waitress is **nicer than** the waiter.

It's **hotter** and **windier** today.

Superlativ

Size 8 is the **smallest** in the shop.

She's the **nicest** person in the office.

It's the **hottest** and **windiest** day of the week.

- An die meisten einsilbigen Adjektive, z. B. *small,* fügt man die Endungen *er* (Komparativ) und *est* (Superlativ): *small → smaller, smallest.*
- Wenn das Adjektiv auf *e* endet, wird nur *r* (Komparativ) bzw. *st* (Superlativ) angehängt: *nice → nicer, nicest.*
- Wenn das Adjektiv auf einen einzelnen Vokal und einen einzelnen Konsonanten endet, wird der Konsonant vor *er* (Komparativ) oder *est* (Superlativ) verdoppelt: *hot → hotter, hottest; big → bigger, biggest.* Das gilt aber **nicht** bei zwei Vokalen (*cool → cooler, coolest*), bei zwei Konsonanten (*warm → warmer, warmest*) und bei *w* oder *y* (*slow → slower, slowest*).
- Bei zweisilbigen Adjektiven, die auf einen Konsonanten + *y* enden, bildet man die Steigerung in der Regel mit *er* und *est.* Dabei wird *y* zu *i* (*windy → windier, windiest; easy → easier, easiest; early → earlier, earliest*).

B THREE-SYLLABLE ADJECTIVES ·
DREISILBIGE ADJEKTIVE

Komparativ

Cookery programmes are OK, but sport is **more interesting**.

The coast is **more beautiful than** the mountains.

Superlativ

This is the **most interesting** building in the town.

We're in the **most beautiful** place in Wales.

- Bei längeren Adjektiven mit drei oder mehr Silben, z. B. *interesting, beautiful,* bildet man die Steigerung mit *more* (Komparativ) und *most* (Superlativ).

C IRREGULAR COMPARISON ·
UNREGELMÄSSIGE STEIGERUNG

Germany has a **good** team – much **better** than England and the **best** in Europe.

The weather was **bad** yesterday, but it's **worse** today. It's the **worst** day of the week.

- Beachten Sie: *good → better, best; bad → worse, worst.*

Transcripts

▶ In diesem Transcript erscheinen nur Hörtexte, die nicht im Hauptteil des Buchers abgedruckt sind.

Die Abkürzung EP in der linken Spalte steht für Extra Practice, die Ziffer (z. B. 07) kennzeichnet die Übung (z. B. Übung 07).

UNIT 2

HAPPY BIRTHDAY!

Spring: March, April, May   Track 06, ex 01
Summer: June, July, August
Autumn: September, October, November
Winter: December, January, February

first, second, third, fourth, fifth, sixth, seventh, eighth, ninth,   Track 08, 04
tenth,
eleventh, twelfth, thirteenth, fourteenth, fifteenth, sixteenth,
seventeenth, eighteenth, nineteenth,
twentieth, twenty-first, twenty-second, twenty-third,
twenty-fourth, twenty-fifth,
twenty-sixth, twenty-seventh, twenty-eighth, twenty-ninth,
thirtieth, thirty-first

1	**Man**	What's this?	Track 12, EP 02
	Woman	It's a cake.	
	Man	A cake? For me?	
	Woman	Yes, of course! It's your birthday. Happy birthday, my love.	

2	**Boy**	Hi Jess! Happy birthday. This is for you.
	Girl	Oh, thanks. OOH I know what this is! Thank you.
	Boy	Let's go in the garden and have a game.
	Girl	Good idea.

3	**Woman**	Happy birthday, Oliver.
	Man	Thank you, granny.
	Woman	Here you are.
	Man	Oh, for me? It's very nice ... er ...
	Woman	Do you like it?
	Man	Yes, yes, I do! I like the colours. Thank you very much.

UNIT 3

I HAVE A RESERVATION

Receptionist	Good afternoon. How can I help you?	Track 15, 10
Mr Sanderson	I have a reservation for a double room for seven nights.	
Receptionist	What's your name, please?	
Mr Sanderson	It's Sanderson. James Sanderson.	
Receptionist	Welcome to our hotel, Mr Sanderson. Do you have any ID?	

Mr Sanderson	Yes, I have my passport.
Receptionist	Great, thank you. Can I check your address, please?
Mr Sanderson	Yes, it's 112 Springhill Road, Lansley in Great Britain.
Receptionist	Super. Do you have a credit card, Mr Sanderson?
Mr Sanderson	Yes, I do. Here you are. How much does a double room with breakfast cost again?
Receptionist	It's 110 euros, sir. Here's your key card. Your room number is 355.
Mr Sanderson	Thank you. Can I ask you something? Is there a swimming pool here?
Receptionist	Yes, there is.
Mr Sanderson	Thank you. And what time is breakfast?
Receptionist	It's from 7 o'clock until 11 o'clock. In the restaurant.
Mr Sanderson	And when is check-out time?
Receptionist	It's 12 o'clock.
Mr Sanderson	Great. Thank you very much.
Receptionist	You're welcome. Enjoy your stay with us.

UNIT 4

GO ALONG THIS ROAD

1 Track 20, 08

	Woman	Oh, excuse me!
	Man	Yes? Can I help you?
	Woman	Is the train station near here?
	Man	Yes, it is. It's in Station Road, opposite the park.
	Woman	Station Road? Oh yes, of course, thank you.
	Man	That's OK.

2

	Woman	Excuse me. How do I find the cinema?
	Girl	The cinema? Er ... Go along York Road. There's a cinema on the left.
	Woman	On York Road?
	Girl	Yes, it's next to an art gallery.
	Woman	Great, thanks!

3

	Woman	Is it far to the supermarket?
	Man	No, it isn't. Go out of the hotel and turn right. Then turn left into Old Street. Go along there, and there's a little supermarket on the right, on the corner of North Street. It's not far.
	Woman	Thank you very much.
	Man	You're welcome.

UNIT 6

THAT LONG, HOT SUMMER

1A cold   **2D** warm   **3B** hot   **4C** sunny   **5F** windy   **6E** wet   Track 25, ex 01

Ben	So, what was it like when you were my age? I mean, there was no internet, right?	Track 28, 09
Grandpa	Yes, that's right. And there weren't any computers in my school. There was a telephone in most houses, but there weren't any mobile phones, of course. And televisions were popular, because that was the only way to watch TV shows or the news. There were no tablets.	
Ben	So, what were computers like in the good old days?	
Grandma	My first computer at work was enormous! I remember, there was a big printer in a different room, for printing letters.	
Ben	What, no email?	
Grandpa	No email. Everything was very slow. People talk about the good old days, but they weren't so good, you know. For example, in those days there weren't any online meetings. So, there were a lot of business trips and a lot of flights.	
Ben	And that wasn't very good for the planet!	

Man	Woah ... oh, hello Frankie! Look Tess, it's your friend Frankie!	Track 30, EP 06
Woman	Oh sorry! Stop that, Frankie ... oh, hi!	
Man	Hello! Nice to see you again!	
Woman	And you! Sorry about Frankie, he's really very friendly!	
Man	I know, it's OK. No problem! What was your holiday like?	
Woman	It was really lovely, thank you. There was a big family party at my parents' house.	
Man	Ah, that's nice. Er ... I can't remember... where do your parents live?	
Woman	In Bremen. It's a city in the north of Germany.	
Man	Ah yes! What was the weather like there?	
Woman	Good. Well, there were two very hot days. But after that, it was cooler and very nice.	
Man	Great!	
Woman	What was it like here?	
Man	Not too bad. There wasn't any rain but there weren't any hot days. You know, just the normal Scottish summer weather!	
Woman	I love your Scottish weather! It's perfect for dog walking ...	

UNIT 7

WE WORKED TOGETHER

Nineteen fifty, nineteen fifty-nine, two thousand, two thousand and nine, twenty ten, twenty eleven, twenty twenty, twenty twenty-four	Track 34, 09

Amy	Granny, when were you born?	Track 35, 10
Charlotte	I was born in 1963. A long long time ago.	
Amy	Yeah! Where were you born?	
Charlotte	In London. My family moved to Bristol when I was 10.	
Amy	Was your school nice?	

Charlotte	Yes, and I loved dancing at school.
Amy	Why?
Charlotte	I don't know. I always wanted to dance.
Amy	Were you a really good dancer?
Charlotte	I was a good dancer, yes. And a good teacher. My first job was in a ballet school. I worked for a man called Carlos. He's famous now.
Amy	Are you famous?
Charlotte	No, but I started a dance studio, in 1990. Charlie's Studio.
Amy	Dad's studio.
Charlotte	Yes, it's your father's studio now.
Amy	And you don't work now.
Charlotte	Well, I'm retired. So I don't teach dancing but I work a lot. I look after a little girl called Amy now ...

Chrissie	It's so nice to see you again, Joss.
Joss	Great to see you too. When were you last on holiday here?
Chrissie	In Switzerland? Two years ago. I went to Zurich. It was my sister's wedding.
Joss	Ah nice. And what was it like?
Chrissie	It was wonderful. We had the best weather possible, and my sister looked beautiful!
Joss	I love weddings!
Chrissie	Me too. I had a great time. What about you?
Joss	Me?
Chrissie	Yes, you travel a lot. When were you last in a different country?
Joss	Let me see ... I went to Brussels for work six months ago, oh and Paris too.
Chrissie	And when were you last in Brazil?
Joss	I went there a year ago, for my daughter's birthday.
Chrissie	Do you miss your family?
Joss	Of course, but I often speak to them and video calls are great.

UNIT 8

WHERE DID YOU STAY?

1   We stayed in an apartment near a lake.
2   We stayed in a bed and breakfast in the city.
3   We stayed at a campsite by the sea.

John	Hello?
Kate	John? Hello it's Kate here.
John	Kate, hi! Are you back?
Kate	Yes, we're home now.
John	Did you enjoy your holiday?
Kate	It was great, thank you.
John	How long were you away?
Kate	Just a week.

John	Thanks for your card. What a beautiful place!
Kate	Oh yes, we loved it.
John	Where did you stay?
Kate	We rented a house near a lake in Hungary.
John	Super. What was it like?
Kate	It wasn't very big, but it was nice. We really liked it.
John	Did you visit many places?
Kate	No, we wanted a quiet holiday. We walked in the mountains a lot.
John	What was the weather like?
Kate	It was sunny and warm for the first five days and then it rained.
John	That's a pity.
Kate	No, it wasn't. It was fine. We stayed at home and cooked some nice meals. And we watched some old films - it was very relaxing.
John	Well that's great ...

		Track 42, EP 01
1	Where did you stay?	
2	What was the weather like?	
3	What did you do when it rained?	
4	Where did you walk?	

UNIT 9

WE HAD A GREAT TIME

buy	bought	Track 43, 01
come	came	
fly	flew	
go	went	
meet	met	
see	saw	
drink	drank	
do	did	
take	took	

Hello from sunny Australia.   Track 45, 09

The weather's great. We flew to Sydney for our first week. We went to the famous Opera House and saw an opera there – that was very special. We did a boat trip too. We took a lot of photos, drank cold beers and had big steaks on the beach. Last week we came to Brisbane, a beautiful city. We bought some nice things for you all.

Love Will.

UNIT 10

CONSOLIDATION

1 **Guest** I don't have the key to my room. I can't find it. **Track 49, 09**
Can you help me, please?

Receptionist Yes, I can give you a key. Just a minute, please.

2 **Felix** Yurek works here. Do you know him?

Basia Not really, but his partner is Sonya. I know her.

3 **Mia** We met two very nice people from Turkey at our hotel. They were really interesting. We went with them and saw the sights. And they came with us to a restaurant for dinner.

Ethan That's cool. Did you enjoy the evening?

Mia Yes, we all enjoyed it very much.

Mum Hello Lisa **Track 50, 10**

Lisa Hi, Mum.

Mum How are you?

Lisa Good thanks.

Mum How's the holiday?

Lisa It's fine. We like it here. It's great.

Mum What about the hotel?

Lisa It isn't a hotel. It's a holiday apartment. It's OK.

Mum Is it expensive?

Lisa No, not really. It doesn't cost very much. And the people are all very friendly.

Mum That's good.

Lisa The problem is the food. I don't like pasta or pizza!

Mum Oh, that's not so good. What's the weather like?

Lisa Ah, the weather is perfect! Nice and hot all the time. And it's a lovely place. There are some lakes here and we swim every day. It's a really great holiday.

UNIT 11

HOW MUCH IS IT?

1 walk **2** cycle **3** go by car **4** go by train **Track 51, 01**
5 go by bus **6** fly **7** go by underground

1 **Assistant** Hello, can I help you? **Track 54, 10**

Man Yes please. A single to Liverpool.

Assistant That's £68.

Man	How much!?	
Assistant	The single is £68.	
Man	Oh! It was much cheaper last year!	

2   Attention please for a platform change. The eleven o'clock train to Liverpool is on platform 3. Platform 3 for the next train to Liverpool.

3

Woman	Are you OK?
Man	Is this platform 1?
Woman	Yes, it is.
Man	Oh but ... is this the train to Liverpool?
Woman	No, it isn't. This is the 10:55 London train. There was a platform change.
Man	Oh. I didn't hear it.
Woman	This train goes to London. The Liverpool train is from platform 3 now.
Man	Really?
Woman	Yes, platform 3.
Man	Thank you very much.
Woman	You're welcome.

Marieke	What about a trip to the shops next week?	**Track 56, EP 02**
Sandy	That's a good idea. I need some new clothes.	
Marieke	Bus or train? What do you think?	
Sandy	The bus is cheaper, but the train is easier. It's half an hour quicker too.	
Marieke	Let's go by train.	
Sandy	OK. How much is a ticket?	
Marieke	I don't know, but I can check on the internet. Sometimes two singles are cheaper than a return.	

1   The next train from Platform 5 is the 14:58 to Manchester.   **Track 57, EP 03**
That's the 14:58 to Manchester from Platform 5.

2   The next train from Platform 2 is the 15:10 to Liverpool. Platform 2 for the 15:10 to Liverpool.

3   The next train from Platform 7 is the 15:13 to Glasgow. The 15:13 to Glasgow from Platform 7.

UNIT 12

IT LOOKS LOVELY!

1

Assistant	Hi, can I help you?	**Track 60, 08**
Young man	Oh yes, please. It's my girlfriend's birthday. She wants a new bag.	
Assistant	A bag. Right ... er ... we sell some nice bags in blue, pink, purple?	
Young man	No, she doesn't like those colours. Do you sell black bags?	
Assistant	I'm not sure ... there's this bag here. It's lovely but ...	

Young man	That's better. I like that. How much does it cost?	
Assistant	That's more expensive. £50.	
Young man	That's fine. Can I have that, please?	
Assistant	Yes of course ...	

2
Assistant	Good afternoon. Can I help you?
Woman	You have a pair of red shoes in the window.
Assistant	Ah yes. What size are you?
Woman	I'm size 39 at home.
Assistant	OK ... that's size 6, here you are.
Woman	Thank you. Yes, they're very comfortable. Oh, and I like this blouse.
Assistant	You can try it on.
Woman	That's a good idea. Where are the changing rooms?
Assistant	Come with me, please ...

Track 62, EP 02

Assistant	Can I help you?
Woman	Yes, can I try on these shoes, please?
Assistant	Yes, of course. How are they?
Woman	Well, I'm not sure. I think they're too small.
Assistant	We have a bigger size here.
Woman	Oh, good. Can I try them on, please? Oh yes, that's better. How much are they?
Assistant	They're £60.
Woman	OK, I'd like them, please.

UNIT 13

I'D LIKE A GARDEN

1 kitchen **2** dining room **3** living room **4** toilet **5** balcony   Track 63, 01
6 bedroom **7** office **8** bathroom

Track 66, 09

Ellie	Granny, we moved to a new house yesterday!
Betty	I know. You're a lucky girl.
Ellie	Why?
Betty	Because you have a big house now.
Ellie	Where did you live when you were young?
Betty	We lived in a flat so we didn't have a garden.
Ellie	Did you have your own room?
Betty	No, I shared a room with my two sisters. The bedroom was always cold.
Ellie	Why?
Betty	We didn't have central heating then.
Ellie	No heating? Did you have a bathroom in your flat?
Betty	Of course we did, but we didn't have a shower in it like you.
Ellie	Did you have a toilet?
Betty	Of course we did! I'm not that old, Ellie!

UNIT 14

I HATE GARDENING

1 reading   **2** cooking   **3** fishing   **4** running   **5** cycling   Track 68, 01
6 gardening   **7** dancing   **8** baking

		Track 71, 08

Lucy   Do you like your coffee black or white?   Track 71, 08
Ahmad   Oh, black please, no milk.
Lucy   Here you are then. So, how many children do you have?
Ahmad   One, Ellie. She's seven. What about you?
Lucy   We have three boys.
Ahmad   Three boys. Wow! Do you go out to work?
Lucy   No, I'm too busy at home. What about you?
Ahmad   I make lunches for offices. I do that in my kitchen. I love cooking.
Lucy   Really? I don't like cooking every day, but I like making cakes. And of
            course the boys love eating them! Do you do any sport?
Ahmad   Uh not really. I like listening to music. Tina tells me your partner likes
            cycling.
Lucy   Oh yes! He goes out every weekend.
Ahmad   Do you go with him?
Lucy   I like cycling but I don't often go.
Ahmad   I love dancing.
Lucy   Me too! Do you like salsa dancing?
Ahmad   Yes, but jazz dancing is easier. I went to a class last year.
Lucy   Jazz dancing? What's that?
Ahmad   It's a dance class with jazz music. It's great, but now I'm too busy.

UNIT 15

CONSOLIDATION

Simon   Where's the waitress? She's very slow. The service here   Track 74, 08
            is the worst in Bristol.
Joel   But the coffee here is very good. It's better than at Lisa's Coffee Shop.
            This is the best place for coffee.
Simon   There's better service at Lisa's, but we can't go there now.
Joel   Yes. Look at the rain. Yesterday was bad, but this is worse.

Video Scripts

Cornwall   Unit 5, p. 47

If you travel South and West in Britain, in the end you will arrive in Cornwall.

You know when you arrive there because many of the place names are different from the rest of Britain. Place names like Pengelly, Polperro, and Trelissick come from the Cornish language. This was the language of the Celtic Britons, and they lived in England before the English-speaking Anglo Saxons arrived. Very few people speak Cornish now, but some people would like it to come back.

Cornwall is different to the rest of Britain in many other ways too. It has the sea on three sides, and the sea has an enormous impact on life in Cornwall.

Fishing is still a major activity. Even the smallest coastal villages have a few local fishing boats. And the port of Newlyn is one of the most important fishing centres in Britain. When you visit Cornwall you should try the local seafood. If you are feeling adventurous, you can buy it like this or like this and cook it yourself.

Or if you prefer, there are many excellent restaurants with fish fresh from the sea, cooked in many different ways. But it isn't easy to find the traditional Cornish Stargazy Pie on many menus these days.

Another traditional Cornish food is clotted cream. The famous Cream Tea has scones with jam and clotted cream. In Cornwall the jam goes on the scone and then the clotted cream goes on top. In other parts of England they often get the order wrong.

But the most famous Cornish dish is of course the Cornish Pasty. This is meat, turnip and potatoes cooked in a pastry case. In the past, it was an easy way for the miners to take their lunch to work down in the tin mines. When the mines closed two hundred years ago, the miners took their mining skills and their pasties all over the world. The ruins of the tin mines are a special part of the Cornish landscape. These mines are on the North Coast of Cornwall and the Coastal Path passes close by.

The coastal path runs high along spectacular cliffs and goes down to beautiful beaches and tiny villages.

The Minack Theatre on the cliffs near Porthcurno is an amazing place to watch a play or an opera. But on some days the weather can make it difficult for the actors and the audience.

Half way along the Coastal Path is Lands End, the South West end of Britain.

At the north end of the path is Tintagel castle. Some people believe that this was the birthplace of King Arthur.

The beautiful landscape, the warm climate, and the romantic history attract many visitors to Cornwall. The landscape, the climate and the history also attract artists and writers. They love to use Cornwall as a subject for their art or a setting for their stories. Rosamunde Pilcher made Cornwall famous, especially in Germany, with her Cornish books. Many of her stories are now popular films on German TV. They bring hundreds of thousands of visitors from Germany to Cornwall each year.

Cornwall always welcomes you! – Cornwall heißt Sie immer willkommen!

Checking into the hotel   Unit 5, p. 47

Receptionist	Guten Tag, wie kann ich Ihnen helfen?
Enrico	Hello. I have a reservation for a single room for two nights. Enrico Rossi.
Receptionist	Thank you, Mr Rossi. Do you have any ID? Passport?
Enrico	Of course, here you are. And my credit card ...
Receptionist	Perfect, thank you. Ah, you are from Italy?
Enrico	Milan, originally, yes.
Receptionist	You speak very good English.
Enrico	I worked in England when I was younger.
Receptionist	I see. There you are, sir, your passport ... and your card.
Enrico	Thanks ... can I ask you something? Am I too late for breakfast?
Receptionist	Ah, I'm very sorry, sir. The kitchen closes at eleven every weekday. It opens again from twelve until two o'clock for lunch. You can get some coffee from the bar.
Enrico	Hmm I need more than a cup of coffee. Are there any good cafés near here?
Receptionist	Oh yes there's a really nice café not far from here. Just go out of the hotel and turn left. Go along to the end, Café Rosalina is on the corner. Opposite the bank.
Enrico	Great, thanks.
Receptionist	Here is your key card, sir. Your room number is 220, on the second floor. The lifts are down that corridor, over there.
Enrico	That's great. Thank you.
Receptionist	Ah, sorry, one moment please. Can you fill [in] this form for me ... your address and contact details. And also the reason for your visit here: private, business ... ?
Enrico	For work. I'm here for the Games Industry Convention.
Receptionist	I see. Very good, sir. Thank you! Enjoy your stay with us!
Enrico	Thank you. Oh, one more thing. Do you have a guest called Steve Newton?
Receptionist	One moment, I can check for you ... no, not yet. But an S. Newton has a reservation for today so ...
Enrico	OK, thanks. When he arrives, please can you give him this.
Receptionist	Of course, not a problem.
Enrico	That's great. Thanks again. Bye, sir.
Receptionist	Have a nice day.
Enrico	Bye bye.

Meeting in the bar   Unit 10, p. 87

Enrico Yes, yes, I checked in this morning. Thank you for making the reservation for me. Yes, it's OK. It's comfortable, nothing special, but everything is OK. Yes, well there is someone called Newton on the list of convention delegates so ... I hope to meet him tonight. Of course. Thanks for calling.

Sam Yeah, I'm here. In a hotel, yeah. Not very interesting. There's nobody interesting here. It's GamesCon, yeah it starts tomorrow. Sure, will do. Bye.

Enrico I could never type so fast.

Sam I'm sorry?

Enrico You write so quickly.

Sam Well yeah ... it's my job.

Enrico I see. What do you do?

Sam I'm a writer. I write interactive storylines ... you know ... computer games ... video games.

Enrico I understand. Do you work for a company?

Sam No, I don't. I'm freelance.

Enrico And you're here for the Games Industry Convention?

Sam Yup.

Enrico Same here.

Sam Really?

Enrico Yes, really! I hope to see an ex-colleague tonight. We worked together years ago...

Sam So you're here for GamesCon, too?

Enrico Yes, I worked for a software development company in the early days of video games. *Super Mario, The Legend of Zelda* ...? You're too young to remember them.

Sam Yeah, those games came out before I was born! But I know them ... my dad worked for Nintendo.

Enrico Your father?!

Sam Yeah he's retired now. But he had a big name in the old days ... together with another guy called Enrico something.

Enrico Rossi. Enrico Rossi. That's me. And you must be ...

Sam I'm Sam Newton. Steve Newton's daughter.

Enrico Well Steve Newton's daughter, I'm very pleased to meet you!

Sam You too, Enrico! Hey, I can't wait to tell my dad ...

In the park   Unit 10, p. 87

Sami	Hello! Oh, sorry ... get down, Sherlock! Don't do that!
Melissa	Hello, Sherlock. Hey, how are you?
Sami	I'm good, thanks. I'm sorry, he's just happy to see you again!
Melissa	We were on vacation. We visited old friends in the UK.
Sami	Nice! And when did you get back?
Melissa	Yesterday. We flew from London Heathrow. It was the last flight, so we were home late.
Sami	And did you enjoy your holiday? Did you have a good time?
Melissa	Oh yes, it was great, thank you.
Sami	Where did you stay?
Melissa	We stayed with my friends most of the time. They live in Bath.
Sami	Sorry, did you say "in the bath"?
Melissa	No, I didn't. I said "in Bath". Bath is a beautiful city in the south west of England.
Sami	Oh right!
Melissa	It's famous for its Roman baths.
Sami	Roman baths? That's cool. Was the weather nice?
Melissa	Not so great. It rained a lot. But we went to London for the last three days and the weather was better there. We stayed in a hotel and went to some shows.
Sami	I love London! It's expensive, but fun! I was there last year.
Melissa	Oh, really? And what did you do this year?
Sami	Oh, I stayed at home. I had a quiet time, but very relaxing. I went swimming and cycling ...
Melissa	That's always nice.
Sami	I went for long walks with the dog of course.
Melissa	And, what was the weather like here?
Sami	It was lovely.
Melissa	Ah, lucky you! And it still is lovely!
Sami	Exactly! Well, come on, Sherlock, time to go home. Good to see you again.
Melissa	Yeah, you too. Bye! Bye Sherlock!

Video 5

The dinner party   **Unit 15, p. 127**

Moritz	What do you think, Tomasina? A tie … or a bow tie?
Tomasina	What?
Moritz	Do you think a tie is better than a bow tie for a dinner party? Hey, you're not ready yet!
Tomasina	No because I don't have anything to wear! I hate going to your chic office parties. I never know what to wear.
Moritz	It's not an office party. It's a dinner party at my boss's house. His wife is English too, she's very nice. Wow, nice dress.
Tomasina	Well you said it was a "fancy" party and to me, "fancy" means "chic". And if it's chic, you can't wear jeans!
Moritz	Oh, really?
Tomasina	Really. How do I look in this? Is it too short? Don't say anything, it is too short. I'm going to try on a different dress. Those trousers are better than the jeans.
Moritz	They're not as comfortable as my jeans but … tie or bow tie? I hate wearing ties.
Tomasina	You're worse than me!
Moritz	Don't take too long – we're going to be late.
Tomasina	What time is the dinner party?
Moritz	Not sure. What does the invitation say?
Tomasina	I don't know! Your boss's very nice English wife sent it to you, not me! How do I look in this? Is it OK?
Moritz	It's great. You look beautiful. Ah here it is! You are invited to a Fancy Dress dinner party at 7 pm on December 28th ….
Tomasina	Fancy Dress party! Did you say: a Fancy Dress Party?! Moritz, that means a costume party!
Moritz	Oh.
Tomasina	Oh no, what are we going to do now? We don't have much time …
Moritz	OK, I have an idea …
Tomasina	What on earth? … Moritz … your old dinner jacket?
Moritz	Let's dress as Miss Sophie and James! *Dinner for one*?
Tomasina	What do you mean, "Dinner for one"?
Moritz	It's a classic comedy sketch. It's on German TV every New Year's Eve – it's a tradition. It has cult status – everyone knows Sir Toby, Mr Pommeroy … it's English, you must know it!
Tomasina	No, I don't, Moritz. I have no idea what you're talking about.
Moritz	That dress is perfect. You can be Miss Sophie, it's her 90th birthday …
Tomasina	Ninetieth?! Great, thanks!
Moritz	No, that's great. Everyone's going to love it. Come on, I can explain it all on the way … I can't believe you don't know *Dinner for one* …

In the apartment   Unit 15, p. 127

Toni	Are you OK, Hetty?
Hetty	Pardon? Sorry, what did you say?
Toni	I know this is hard for you. Are you all right?
Hetty	Yes, thanks Toni. I was in a dream. I'm fine. It's just that …
Toni	I understand. Your parents lived here for many years, didn't they?
Hetty	All their married life, yes, And I grew up in this apartment. I'm sure my mother was very sad when she left this place – her home.
Toni	Yes but now she is happy, you know that.
Hetty	Yes. It's a very nice care home. They look after her well and she is more comfortable than she was here. There are no stairs, there's a lovely garden and she loves sitting outside. She always has people she can talk to …
Toni	Exactly. So now, what do we do with this place?
Hetty	The balcony is lovely … look. I mean, this is a beautiful apartment, and it's probably bigger than our house.
Toni	It's very big!
Hetty	I know, and we don't need so many rooms … or so much furniture. I really love our house, I don't want to live in the city. This kitchen is very small and I really like cooking … so …
Toni	So what's the answer? Your mother can't live here, and you don't want to …
Hetty	No, I don't. But I want to keep it in the family, I don't want to sell it.
Toni	OK so what about … why don't we rent it out?
Hetty	Rent it?
Toni	I mean, let's change it … into an Airbnb. Or rent it to students. Or a family for short stays.
Hetty	An Airbnb?
Toni	Well, I don't know how that works but why not? This is a perfect location for visitors to the city, isn't it?
Hetty	Yes, it is, that's true, and … and people rent out apartments much smaller than this.
Toni	It has too much furniture, of course.
Hetty	People need sofas and chairs, beds, cupboards … maybe not so much of everything.
Toni	What do you think?
Hetty	I don't know, Toni, it's a lot of work, but … OK … let's do it!

Answer Key: Facts & Fun

Unit 2   **Page 23**

Z	N	N	K	H	A	N	U	K	K	A	H
K	B	E	E	A	W	J	K	S	I	T	E
D	I	W	C	H	R	I	S	T	M	A	S
O	R	Y	C	U	G	D	J	Z	L	Z	K
E	T	E	M	J	K	F	W	F	W	F	V
T	H	A	N	K	S	G	I	V	I	N	G
Q	D	R	E	I	D	A	L	F	I	T	R
P	A	X	L	P	Y	J	A	H	Y	L	W
H	Y	I	B	O	X	I	N	G	D	A	Y

Unit 3   **Page 31**

in, lot, can, ace, act, arc, car, can't, cola, continent, hotel etc.

Unit 4   **Page 39**

pharmacy, post office, cinema, bookshop
café, pub, newsagent's, cash machine

Unit 6   **Page 55**

1 windy, **2** lovely, **3** rain, **4** hot, **5** night, **6** early, **7** summer

Unit 9   **Page 79**

the wheel, the train, the telephone, the plane, the television, the computer

Unit 12   **Page 103**

2, 1, 3

Unit 14   **Page 119**

1   autumn
2   in Bristol
3   in Sydney
4   Oxford Street

Answer Key: Video Exercises

Video 1   **1** C   **2** B   **3** A   **4** C

Video 2   **1** his passport and credit card
2 from Milan in Italy; he worked in England when he was younger
3 it opens from 12 to 2
4 it's room 220 on the second floor
5 the reason for his visit: private or business
6 it falls off the reception desk

Video 3   **1 A** Sam   **B** Enrico   **C** Sam   **D** Enrico   **E** Sam   **F** Sam
2 Because to her, he is an old man and not interesting.
3 Because he thinks he is meeting her father, his ex-colleague Steve.

Video 4   **1** To Sherlock: Get down, Sherlock! / Don't do that! To Melissa: I'm sorry, he's just happy to see you again.
2 A yesterday   **B** with friends   **C** likes   **D** at home   **E** worse
3 Melissa says she stayed in Bath, a beautiful city in the south west of England (famous for its Roman Baths).

Video 5   **1** C   **2** A   **3** C   **4** B

Video 6   **1** False. Toni understands Hetty very well.
2 True.
3 False. Hetty knows the care home is good for her mother.
4 True.
5 False. Hetty loves cooking but her mother's old kitchen is too small.
6 True.

Answer Key: Extra Practice

Unit 1

01
1 watch TV
2 eat a meal
3 ask a question
4 play a game
5 meet friends
6 buy a present

02 **A**4 **B**1 **C**6 **D**3 **E**5 **F**2

03
1 Darius has breakfast at six o'clock.
2 He is busy at the moment.
3 Darius finishes work at eleven or twelve.
4 His parents look after their grandchildren on weekdays.
5 The children wake up early every morning.
6 He doesn't drive a taxi at the weekend.

04
1 He cooks in a restaurant.
2 She drives a taxi.
3 She looks after old people.
4 She works in a supermarket.
5 She checks passports.

05
1 I don't eat
2 I don't have
3 She doesn't have
4 where do you go?
5 Do you know
6 Does it have
7 the food doesn't cost

Unit 2

01
1 the second of May
2 the twenty-third of May
3 the eleventh of June
4 the twelfth of June
5 the seventh of July
6 the thirtieth of July

02 **1**C **2**A **3**D

03 **1**D **2**C **3**B **4**A

04
1 Nick often has lunch in the office.
2 She sometimes works at weekends.
3 She never eats out at lunchtime.
4 Nick often finishes work early on Friday.
5 They sometimes have an online party.
6 Sheila never enjoys parties.
7 Darius always gets up early.

05 **1** let's **2** pity **3** special **4** here **5** word **6** surprise **7** idea

Unit 3

01
1 afternoon C
2 breakfast B
3 grandson A
4 passport E
5 policeman D
6 post code G
7 weekend F

02
1 a cup **2** some chips **3** some soup **4** a dress **5** some wine **6** some bottles
7 a glass **8** some luggage **9** some keys

03 **1** A **2** E **3** B **4** D **5** C

04
1 Where is the breakfast room?
2 Do you take credit cards?
3 Is there a sauna here?
4 Is there a bus or train from here?
5 What time is the next train?
6 How much does a taxi cost?

05 to / How / have / single / What's / Do / floor / What / from / some / your

Unit 4

01
1 The hotel is on the right. It's next to the supermarket.
2 The art gallery is on the left. It's next to the museum.
3 The theatre is on the left. It's next to the swimming pool.
4 The bookshop is on the right. It's next to the pharmacy.

02
1 way **2** far **3** out **4** left **5** along **6** cinema **7** straight **8** traffic light
9 left **10** Middle **11** right

03 **1** D **2** E **3** A **4** F **5** C **6** B

04
1 You need some money? Go to a bank.
2 You need a nice meal? Go to a restaurant.
3 You need a drink? Go to a bar.
4 You need a ticket? Go to the station.

05
5 There are four seasons in a year.
6 There are 24 hours in a day.
7 There are twelve months in a year.
8 There are thirty-one days in March.

06 → **1** at, **2** with, **3** from, **6** near, **8** in, **9** of, **10** out, **11** to
↓ **1** after, **3** for, **4** on, **5** into, **6** next, **7** about

Unit 6

01 **1** It's hot **2** It's wet. **3** It's windy. **4** It's cold.

02
A We were at the balloon fiesta yesterday.
B Oh, really, was it good?
A It was great. There were lots of people.
B And were there many balloons?
A Yes, hundreds of balloons. You must go and see them.
B Yes, why not? I can go on Saturday.

03
1 I was in Hong Kong three years ago.
2 I was with William five years ago.
3 I was in London a week ago.
4 We were new in town twelve years ago.

04 1 were 2 Were 3 wasn't 4 wasn't 5 was 6 were
7 weren't 8 was 9 wasn't

05 1 wasn't 2 were, was 3 was, wasn't 4 was, were 5 were

06 1C 2D 3A 4E 5B

Unit 7

01 2, 4, 5, 7, 9

02 niece, son, brother, grandfather, uncle, nephew, daughter, sister

03 1 was 2 lived 3 moved 4 was 5 worked 6 died 7 visited 8 walked
9 remembered 10 were

04
1 In the morning she looked after her granddaughter.
2 Then she phoned a friend
3 In the afternoon she played tennis.
4 In the evening she cooked a meal.
5 Then she watched TV.

05 1 two 2 sister's 3 six 4 daughter's

06
1 It's his favourite season.
2 It's her favourite colour.
3 It's his favourite drink.
4 It's her favourite sport.
5 It's his favourite meal.
6 He's their favourite uncle.

Unit 8

01
1 We stayed in a camper van.
2 It rained every day.
3 We watched TV in the camper van.
4 We walked on the beach.

02
1 What's the hotel like?
2 What was the food like?
3 What's the beach like?
4 What was the concert like?

03
1 They didn't rent a camper van.
2 They didn't like the house.
3 They didn't stay two weeks.
4 They didn't book last minute.
5 They didn't play football.
6 They didn't visit museums.

04 1 Yes, we did 2 No, she doesn't. 3 Yes, we do.
4 Yes, she does. 5 No, I didn't. 6 No, they don't.

05
1 Sorry? When did you visit?
2 Sorry? What did the children play?
3 Sorry? When did you start the job?
4 Sorry? Where did Sam live?

06 1 cinema 2 Switzerland 3 autumn 4 aunt 5 expensive 6 eat

Unit 9

01 1 train 2 meal 3 waiter 4 friendly 5 trip 6 happy
7 famous 8 yesterday 9 beach 10 clean 11 quiet 12 week

02 1G 2D 3F 4A 5B 6C 7H 8E

03 1 he flew 2 they came 3 we went 4 she drank
5 he bought 6 I met 7 I took 8 she ate

04 1 Chris and his wife flew to Switzerland.
2 They didn't go by car.
3 They had fondue.
4 They didn't drink German wine.
5 They bought some postcards.
6 Emma's family did a tour of a castle.
7 It didn't rain a lot.
8 The children played on the beach.
9 The dog didn't go into the sea.

05 1 booked 2 went 3 came 4 bought 5 took
6 visited 7 flew 8 turned 9 looked

Unit 11

01 1 Our teacher went to Paris by train.
2 My friend went to Zurich by car.
3 Flora went to Glasgow by bus.
4 Daniel went to the airport by taxi.

02 1 idea 2 think 3 quicker 4 easier 5 Let's 6 much 7 know 8 return

03 My train leaves at 15:10 from platform 2.

04 1 The bus is cheaper than the train.
2 February is colder than July.
3 Friday is nicer than Monday.
4 Germany is bigger than Poland.
5 English is easier than French.
6 6 a.m. is earlier than 6 p.m.

05 1 grandparents, parents, grandchildren
2 summer, autumn, winter
3 morning, lunchtime, afternoon, evening
4 town, building, room, bus
5 year, month, week, day, hour, minute

Unit 12

01 1 We can buy him a pullover.
2 Let's buy her a book.
3 We can buy her a football.
4 Let's buy him theatre tickets.
5 We can buy him a birthday cake.

02
1. Can I help you?
2. Yes, can I try on these shoes, please?
3. Yes, of course. How are they?
4. Well, I'm not sure. I think they're too small.
5. We have a bigger size here.
6. Oh, good. Can I try them on, please?
7. Oh yes, that's better. How much are they?
8. They're £60.
9. OK, I'd like them, please.

03
1. I need a cheaper scarf.
2. I need a longer jacket.
3. I need a bigger bag.
4. I need a later train.

04 **1** for **2** with **3** than **4** at **5** on

05 **1** E **2** D **3** B **4** A **5** C

06 **1** nicest **2** most interesting **3** most popular **4** oldest **5** worst

Unit 13

01 **1** living room **2** kitchen **3** dining room **4** bedroom **5** bathroom

02
Rooms: bathroom, kitchen, toilet
Buildings: castle, church, house
Meals: breakfast, dinner, lunch
Relatives: nephew, parent, sister
Weather: hot, sunny, wet

03
1. She buys a lot of dresses.
2. She watches a lot of series.
3. He plays a lot of games.
4. They visit a lot of places.
5. They drink a lot of red wine.

04
1. There aren't many guests at the hotel.
2. There isn't much food in the kitchen.
3. There aren't many rooms in the flat.
4. There isn't much money in my jacket.

05 **1** How much **2** How many **3** How many **4** How much

06 **1** Church Street **2** Park Road **3** Albert Road **4** King Street **5** Victoria Road

Unit 14

01
1. He likes gardening.
2. They like walking.
3. They like shopping.
4. He likes swimming.
5. They like eating out.
6. She likes cycling.

02 **1** likes cooking **2** eat out **3** dancing **4** come **5** filling in
6 working **7** moved into **8** gets up **9** try on **10** going

03 **1** C **2** B **3** D **4** A **5** E **6** F

04 **1** next door **2** place **3** bike **4** sister **5** clothes **6** storey

05 **1** wife **2** shower **3** awful **4** working **5** of course **6** staff **7** single **8** hate

Unit Word List

Verwendete Abkürzungen

AE	amerikanisches Englisch	jds	jemandes
etw	etwas	pl	Plural
EP	Extra Practice	S	Summary
jd	jemand	sb	somebody
jdm	jemandem	sth	something
jdn	jemanden	R	Review

UNIT 1   I have two jobs

1 to **introduce oneself** [ˌɪntrəˈdjuːs wʌnself] — sich vorstellen

Iran [ɪˈrɑːn] — Iran

to **live** [lɪv] — leben, wohnen

company [ˈkʌmpəni] — Firma, Unternehmen

care home [ˈkeə həʊm] — Pflegeheim

to **drive** [draɪv] — fahren

2 to **get up** [ˌget ˈʌp] — aufstehen

to **have lunch** [həv ˈlʌntʃ] — zu Mittag essen

a lot of [ə ˈlɒt əv] — viel(e)

3 **daily routine** [ˌdeɪli ruːˈtiːn] — Tagesablauf

to **have breakfast** [həv ˈbrekfəst] — frühstücken

to **go shopping** [gəʊ ˈʃɒpɪŋ] — einkaufen gehen

gym [dʒɪm] — Fitness-Studio

4 to **take sb somewhere** [ˌteɪk ˈsʌmweə] — jdn wohin bringen

to **take sth** [teɪk] — etw nehmen

bag [bæg] — (Reise-)Tasche, Koffer, Beutel

heavy [ˈhevi] — schwer

where to? [ˌweə ˈtuː] — wohin?

near [nɪə] — in der Nähe von, nahe (bei)

to **know sb/sth** [nəʊ] — jdn/etw kennen

wife [waɪf] — (Ehe-)Frau

part-time [ˌpɑːˈtaɪm] — Teilzeit-

to **go to school** [ˌgəʊ tə ˈskuːl] — in die / zur Schule gehen

baby girl [ˌbeɪbi ˈgɜːl] — kleines Mädchen (im Säuglingsalter)

That's hard work! [ðæts ˌhɑːd ˈwɜːk] — Das ist (ganz schön) viel Arbeit!

late [leɪt] — spät, zu spät

to **work late** [wɜːk ˈleɪt] — spät / bis in die Nacht arbeiten

day job [ˈdeɪ dʒɒb] — Hauptberuf, Job für den Lebensunterhalt

money [ˈmʌni] — Geld, hier: Bezahlung

driver [ˈdraɪvə] — Fahrer/in

from 8 o'clock [frəm ˌeɪt əˈklɒk] — ab 8 Uhr

to **finish** [ˈfɪnɪʃ] — aufhören, Feierabend machen

busy day [ˌbɪsi ˈdeɪ] — arbeitsreicher / langer Tag

easy [ˈiːzi] — einfach, leicht

next door [ˌnekst ˈdɔː] — nebenan

retired [rɪˈtaɪəd] — im Ruhestand

student teacher [ˌstjuːdnt ˈtiːtʃə] — Referendar/in

(job) interview [ˈɪntəvjuː] — Vorstellungsgespräch

Good luck! [ˌgʊd ˈlʌk] — Viel Glück!

Perfect! [ˈpɜːfɪkt] — Sehr gut! Prima!

5 **early** [ˈɜːli] — früh

6 **grandson** [ˈgrænsʌn] — Enkel

7 to **wake up** [ˌweɪk ˈʌp] — aufwachen

to **teach** [tiːtʃ] — unterrichten

grandparents pl [ˈgrænpeərənts] — Großeltern

on weekdays [ˌɒn ˈwiːkdeɪz] — unter der Woche, wochentags

8 to **look after sb** [lʊk ˈɑːftə] — sich um jdn kümmern

10 **table** [ˈteɪbl] — Tabelle

at lunchtime [ˈlʌntʃtaɪm] — mittags, zur Mittagszeit

evening meal [ˈiːvnɪŋ miːl] — Abendessen, Abendbrot

class [klɑːs] — Kurs

EP2 to **watch TV** [ˌwɒtʃ tiː ˈviː] — fernsehen

then [ðen]	anschließend, dann	
EP3 to **be busy** [bi ˈbɪzi]	(viel) zu tun haben, beschäftigt sein	
EP4 **passport** [ˈpɑːspɔːt]	Reisepass	
supermarket [ˈsuːpəmɑːkɪt]	Supermarkt	

In the office...?

Excuse me, where can I find...?	Entschuldigung, wo kann ich ... finden?
Here we are.	Wir sind da / Da sind wir.
Visitor for you!	Besuch für Sie/dich/euch!
Do you eat out?	Essen Sie/isst du/esst ihr auswärts?
I'm so busy. – Me too!	Ich habe so viel zu tun! – Ich auch!

UNIT 2   Happy birthday!

1 **season** [ˈsiːzn]	Jahreszeit	
spring [sprɪŋ]	Frühling	
summer [ˈsʌmə]	Sommer	
autumn [ˈɔːtəm]	Herbst	
March [mɑːtʃ]	März	
May [meɪ]	Mai	
June [dʒuːn]	Juni	
July [dʒuˈlaɪ]	Juli	
October [ɒkˈtəʊbə]	Oktober	
December [dɪˈsembə]	Dezember	
January [ˈdʒænjuəri]	Januar	
February [ˈfebruəri]	Februar	
2 **favourite** [ˈfeɪvərɪt]	Lieblings-, liebste/r/s	
What about you? [ˌwɒt əbaʊt ˈjuː]	Was ist mit dir/euch/Ihnen? Und du/Sie?	
month [mʌnθ]	Monat	
4 **first** [fɜːst]	erste/r/s	
second [ˈsekənd]	zweite/r/s	
third [θɜːd]	dritte/r/s	
fourth [fɔːθ]	vierte/r/s	
7 to **have a party** [həv ə ˈpɑːti]	feiern, eine Party geben	
usually [ˈjuːʒuəli]	normalerweise, üblicherweise, gewöhnlich	
special [ˈspeʃl]	besonders, außergewöhnlich; besondere/r/s, Sonder-	

Christmas [ˈkrɪsməs]	Weihnachten	
Chinese [tʃaɪˈniːz]	chinesisch	
New Year [njuː ˈjɪə]	Neujahr	
to **know** [nəʊ]	wissen	
never [ˈnevə]	nie	
That's a pity! [ˌðæts ə ˈpɪti]	Schade! Wie schade!	
to **enjoy sth** [ɪnˈdʒɔɪ]	etw genießen, etw mögen	
Same here. [ˌseɪm ˈhɪə]	Ebenso. Ich auch.	
to **invite sb (to sth)** [ɪnˈvaɪt]	jdn (zu etw) einladen	
surprise [səˈpraɪz]	Überraschung	
colleague [ˈkɒliːg]	Kollege/-in	
8 **sometimes** [ˈsʌmtaɪmz]	manchmal	
to **plan sth** [plæn]	etw planen	
10 **Europe** [ˈjʊərəp]	Europa	
station [ˈsteɪʃn]	Bahnhof	
11 to **be true for sb** [bi ˈtruː fə]	auf jdn zutreffen	
vegetarian [ˌvedʒəˈteəriən]	vegetarisch	
to **swim** [swɪm]	schwimmen	
beer garden [ˈbɪə gɑːdn]	Biergarten	
to **go for a walk** [ˌgəʊ fər ə ˈwɔːk]	spazieren gehen	
EP2 **granny** [ˈgræni]	Oma, Omi	
EP4 to **eat out** [ˌiːt ˈaʊt]	essen gehen, außerhalb essen	

I usually ...

I never have a birthday party.	Ich feiere meinen Geburtstag nie.
– That's a pity.	– Das ist aber schade!
I usually work late.	Ich arbeite normalerweise (bis) spätabends.
– Same here.	– Ich auch.
I often / sometimes leave early too.	Oft / Manchmal gehe ich auch früher.
I always give her a surprise.	Ich bereite ihr immer eine Überraschung.
– I won't say a word to her!	– Ich sag ihr kein Wort!

UNIT 3   I have a reservation

1 **reservation** [ˌrezəˈveɪʃn]	Reservierung	
business trip [ˈbɪznəs trɪp]	Geschäftreise	
to **check in** [ˌtʃek ˈɪn]	einchecken, sich anmelden	

receptionist [rɪˈsepʃənɪst]	Empfangschef/-dame, Rezeptionist/in
room [ruːm]	Zimmer, Raum
single room [ˌsɪŋgl ˈruːm]	Einzelzimmer
Ms [mɪz]	(Anrede:) Frau
any [ˈeni]	(irgend)ein/e
ID [ˌaɪ ˈdiː]	Ausweis
2 **double room**	Doppelzimmer
[ˌdʌbl ˈruːm]	
3 **night** [naɪt]	Nacht
ID card [ˌaɪ ˈdiː kɑːd]	Personalausweis
to **fill sth in** [ˌfɪl ˈɪn]	etw ausfüllen
form [fɔːm]	Formular
of course [əf ˈkɔːs]	natürlich, selbstverständlich
to **pay** [peɪ]	zahlen, bezahlen
Indian [ˈɪndiən]	indisch
café [ˈkæfeɪ]	Café
free [friː]	kostenlos, gratis
guest [gest]	Gast
key [kiː]	Schlüssel
key card [ˈkiː kɑːd]	Schlüsselkarte
floor [flɔː]	Etage, Stock(werk)
some [sʌm]	einige, ein paar
over there [ˌəʊvə ˈðeə]	da/dort drüben, dahinten
until [ənˈtɪl]	bis
luggage [ˈlʌgɪdʒ]	Gepäck
help [help]	Hilfe
6 **Russian** [ˈrʌʃn]	russisch
7 **sightseeing** [ˈsaɪtsiːɪŋ]	Besichtigung(en) (von Sehenswürdigkeiten)
tired [ˈtaɪəd]	müde
8 to **clean sth** [kliːn]	etw reinigen, etw säubern
to **travel** [ˈtrævl]	reisen
Ireland [ˈaɪələnd]	Irland
9 to **go dancing**	tanzen gehen
[ˌgəʊ ˈdɑːnsɪŋ]	
10 **Great Britain**	Großbritannien
[ˌgreɪt ˈbrɪtn]	
check-out [ˈtʃekaʊt]	Abreise, Auschecken
stay [steɪ]	Aufenthalt
with sb [wɪð, wɪθ]	bei jdm
Enjoy your stay!	Angenehmen Aufenthalt!
[ɪnˌdʒɔɪ jɔː ˈsteɪ]	
surname [ˈsɜːneɪm]	Nachname, Familienname
EP3 to **leave sth** [liːv]	etw verlassen
information [ˌɪnfəˈmeɪʃn]	Angaben
EP5 **That's fine.** [ˌðæts ˈfaɪn]	Das ist (völlig) okay.

I have a reservation

How can I help you?	Wie kann ich Ihnen/dir/ euch behilflich sein?
– I have a reservation for a single room / for two nights.	– Ich habe eine Reservierung für ein Einzelzimmer / für zwei Nächte.
Do you have any ID / a credit card?	Haben Sie irgendeinen Ausweis / eine Kreditkarte (dabei)?
Do you take American Express? – Sorry, sir, we don't.	Nehmen Sie American Express? – Tut mir leid (, mein Herr), die nehmen wir nicht.
Can you fill in this registration form for me, please?	Können Sie bitte dieses Anmeldeformular für mich ausfüllen?
Do you need any help? – Where can I leave my car?	Kann ich Ihnen/dir/euch irgendwie behilflich sein? – Wo kann ich mein Auto lassen?
When is breakfast?	Wann gibt es Frühstück?
When is checkout time?	Bis wann müssen die Zimmer geräumt sein?

UNIT 4 Go along this road

along [əˈlɒŋ]	entlang
road [rəʊd]	(Land-)Straße
1 **reception** [rɪˈsepʃn]	Empfang, Rezeption
pharmacy [ˈfɑːməsi]	Apotheke
art [ɑːt]	Kunst
gallery [ˈgæləri]	Galerie
newsagent's	Zeitschriftenladen, Kiosk
[ˈnjuːzeɪdʒənts]	
bookshop [ˈbʊkʃɒp]	Buchhandlung
near here [nɪə ˈhɪə]	hier in der Nähe
to **turn right/left**	rechts/links abbiegen
[ˌtɜːn ˈraɪt/ˈleft]	
into [ˈɪntə]	in, in … hinein
on the right/left	auf der rechten/linken
[ɒn ðə ˈraɪt/ˈleft]	Seite
street [striːt]	Straße
2 **straight on** [ˌstreɪt ˈɒn]	geradeaus
corner [ˈkɔːnə]	Ecke
on the corner	an der Ecke
[ɒn ðə ˈkɔːnə]	
next to [ˈnekst tə]	neben
opposite [ˈɒpəzɪt]	gegenüber

4 **cash mashine** ['kæʃ məʃiːn] — Geldautomat

lion ['laɪən] — Löwe

traffic lights *pl* ['træfɪk laɪts] — Ampel

map [mæp] — (Land-)Karte, (Stadt-)Plan

8 **train station** ['treɪn steɪʃn] — Bahnhof

10 **Irish** ['aɪrɪʃ] — irisch

12 **directions** *pl* [dəˈrekʃnz] — Wegbeschreibung

EP2 **shop assistant** ['ʃɒp əsɪstənt] — Verkäufer/in

EP6 **choir** ['kwaɪə] — Chor

Go along this road

Can you tell me the way from here? — Können Sie/kannst du/ könnt ihr mir den Weg erklären?

Is there a ... near here? — Gibt es hier in der Nähe einen/eine/ein ...?

There's a ... on the left. — Da ist ein/eine ... auf der linken Seite.

Turn into ... / right. — Biegen Sie/bieg/biegt in ... ein / rechts ab.

It's next to a ... / opposite the ... — Es ist neben einem/einer ... / gegenüber dem/ der...

Go along ... / straight on. — Gehen Sie/geh/geht ... entlang / geradeaus.

... is on the corner. — ...ist an der Ecke.

Sorry, I'm not from here. — Tut mir leid, ich bin nicht von hier.

Is it far? — Ist das weit?

UNIT 5   Consolidation

1 **tourist** ['tʊərɪst] — Tourist/in

tourist information [ˌtʊərɪst ɪnfəˈmeɪʃn] — Touristeninformation

city centre [ˌsɪti ˈsentə] — Stadtzentrum, Innenstadt

visitor ['vɪzɪtə] — Besucher/in, Gast

event [ɪˈvent] — Veranstaltung

balloon [bəˈluːn] — Ballon

for example [fər ɪgˈzɑːmpl] — zum Beispiel

to **end** [end] — enden

outside ['aʊtsaɪd] — außerhalb (von), vor

popular ['pɒpjələ] — beliebt

half [hɑːf] — halbe/r/s

half a million [ˌhɑːf ə ˈmɪljən] — eine halbe Million

4 **on the waterfront** [ɒn ðə ˈwɔːtəfrʌnt] — am Ufer, am Wasser

life [laɪf] — Leben

8 **leaflet** ['liːflət] — Faltblatt, Prospekt, Broschüre

timetable ['taɪmteɪbl] — Fahrplan

attraction [əˈtrækʃn] — Sehenswürdigkeit, Attraktion

11 to **get somewhere** ['get sʌmweə] — wohin kommen, wohin gelangen

R **Dear ...,** [dɪə] — Liebe/r ...,

to **confirm sth** [kənˈfɜːm] — etw bestätigen

booking ['bʊkɪŋ] — Buchung, Reservierung

included [ɪnˈkluːdɪd] — inbegriffen

Best regards, [ˌbest rɪˈgɑːdz] — Mit freundlichen Grüßen

One person

One person – two people — Eine Person – zwei Personen

One man – five men — Ein Mann – fünf Männer

One woman – two women — Eine Frau – zwei Frauen

One child – some children — Ein Kind – einige Kinder

UNIT 6   That long, hot summer

1 **long** [lɒŋ] — lang

cold [kəʊld] — kalt

sunny ['sʌni] — sonnig

wet [wet] — nass, feucht

windy ['wɪndi] — windig

2 **lovely** ['lʌvli] — schön, nett, wunderbar

was [wɒz] — war

yesterday ['jestədeɪ] — gestern

You're right. [jɔː ˈraɪt] — Du hast / Ihr habt recht.

awful ['ɔːfl] — furchtbar, fürchterlich

last [lɑːst] — letzte/r/s

last night [lɑːst ˈnaɪt] — gestern Abend

3 **weather** ['weðə] — Wetter

4 **were** [wɜː] — warst, wart, waren

the good old days *pl* [ðə ˌgʊd əʊld ˈdeɪz] — die gute alte Zeit, die guten alten Zeiten

to **remember** [rɪˈmembə] — sich erinnern

only [ˈəʊnli]	nur	**slow** [sləʊ]	langsam
then [ðen]	damals	**meeting** [ˈmiːtɪŋ]	Besprechung, Sitzung
best [best]	beste/r/s	**flight** [flaɪt]	Flug
(12 years) ago [əˈgəʊ]	vor (12 Jahren)	**planet** [ˈplænɪt]	Planet
both [bəʊθ]	beide	10 **memory** [ˈmeməri]	Erinnerung
young [jʌŋ]	jung	**boyfriend** [ˈbɔɪfrend]	Freund
different [ˈdɪfrənt]	anders	**girlfriend** [ˈgɜːlfrend]	Freundin
to **be with sb** [bi wɪð]	mit jdm zusammen sein	S to **be friends** [bi ˈfrendz]	befreundet sein
married (to sb) [ˈmærid]	(mit jdm) verheiratet	**together** [təˈgeðə]	zusammen
for (6 years) [fə]	(6 Jahre) lang	to **be late** [bi ˈleɪt]	sich verspäten, spät dran sein
divorced [dɪˈvɔːst]	geschieden		
back [bæk]	(wieder) zurück, wieder	EP2 **lots of** [ˈlɒts əv]	viel(e), eine Menge
United States of America (USA)	Vereinigte Staaten von Amerika	EP4 **detective** [dɪˈtektɪv]	Kriminalbeamter/-beamtin
[juˌnaɪtɪd ˌsteɪts əv əˈmerɪkə]		EP5 to **be early** [bi ˈɜːli]	zu früh sein, früh dran sein
happy [ˈhæpi]	zufrieden, glücklich	EP6 **Scottish** [ˈskɒtɪʃ]	schottisch
America [əˈmerɪkə]	Amerika	to **walk the dog**	den Hund ausführen, mit dem Hund spazieren gehen
to **miss sb/sth** [mɪs]	jdn/etw vermissen	[ˌwɔːk ðə ˈdɒg]	
rain [reɪn]	Regen		
house [haʊs]	Haus	**Scotland** [ˈskɒtlənd]	Schottland
to **drink to sb/sth**	auf jdn/etw trinken, auf jdn/etw anstoßen		
[ˈdrɪŋk tə]			
Sure. [ʃʊə]	Na klar!	**The weather**	
7 **better** [ˈbetə]	besser	*It's a lovely day. – Yes, it's …*	Heute ist ein herrlicher Tag. – Ja, es ist …
late [leɪt]	verspätet, zu spät	*… warm / hot / sunny.*	…warm / heiß / sonnig.
8 **What was the weather like?**	Wie war das Wetter?	*… cold / wet / windy.*	…kalt / nass / windig.
		… nice / great / awful.	…schön / toll / furchtbar.
[ˌwɒt wəz ðə ˌweðə ˈlaɪk]			
holiday [ˈhɒlədeɪ]	Urlaub, Ferien		
9 **past** [pɑːst]	Vergangenheit		
age [eɪdʒ]	Alter	**UNIT 7 We worked together**	
to **be sb's age**	in jds Alter sein	1 **born** [bɔːn]	geboren
[bi ˌsʌmbədiz ˈeɪdʒ]		3 to **move to …** [ˈmuːv tə]	nach … ziehen
to **mean** [miːn]	meinen	**relative** [ˈrelətɪv]	Verwandte/r
grandpa [ˈgræmpɑː]	Opa	to **die** [daɪ]	sterben
most [məʊst]	die meisten	**last** [lɑːst]	zuletzt, das letzte Mal
television [ˈtelɪvɪʒn]	Fernseher	**possible** [ˈpɒsəbl]	möglich
popular [ˈpɒpjələ]	(allgemein) verbreitet	**video call** [ˈvɪdiəʊ kɔːl]	Videogespräch
the only way	die einzige Möglichkeit	**mum** [mʌm]	Mama
[ði ˌəʊnli ˈweɪ]		**United Kingdom (UK)**	Vereinigtes Königreich, Großbritannien
TV show [ˌtiː ˈviː ʃəʊ]	Fernsehsendung	[juˌnaɪtɪd ˈkɪŋdəm]	
news *pl* [njuːz]	Nachrichten	**newspaper** [ˈnjuːzpeɪpə]	Zeitung
enormous [ɪˈnɔːməs]	riesig, enorm (groß)	**reporter** [rɪˈpɔːtə]	Reporter/in
printer [ˈprɪntə]	Drucker	**smart** [smɑːt]	intelligent, klug, schlau
different [ˈdɪfrənt]	andere/r/s	**boss** [bɒs]	Chef/in
to **print sth** [prɪnt]	etw drucken, etw ausdrucken	**photographer** [fəˈtɒgrəfə]	Fotograf/in
		answer [ˈɑːnsə]	Antwort
letter [ˈletə]	Brief	**nephew** [ˈnevjuː]	Neffe
everything [ˈevriθɪŋ]	alles	**niece** [niːs]	Nichte

banker [ˈbæŋkə]	Bankkaufmann/-frau, Banker/in	
to **change sth** [tʃeɪndʒ]	etw wechseln	
farmer [ˈfɑːmə]	Bauer/Bäuerin, Farmer/in	
6 to **phone sb** [fəʊn]	jdn anrufen	
8 to **email sb** [ˈiːmeɪl]	jdm eine Email schicken	
aunt [ɑːnt]	Tante	
10 to **dance** [dɑːns]	tanzen	
dancer [ˈdɑːnsə]	Tänzer/in	
ballet [ˈbæleɪ]	Ballett	
called [kɔːld]	namens	
to **start sth** [stɑːt]	etw (Firma usw.) gründen	
dance studio	Tanzstudio, Tanzschule	
[ˈdɑːns stjuːdiəʊ]		
12 **castle** [ˈkɑːsl]	Burg, Schloss	
true [truː]	wahr	
EP5 **Switzerland** [ˈswɪtsələnd]	(die) Schweiz	
went [went]	*Simple past von* to go	
Zurich [ˈzjʊərɪk]	Zürich	
wedding [ˈwedɪŋ]	Hochzeit	
to **look** [lʊk]	aussehen	
beautiful [ˈbjuːtɪfl]	schön	
Brussels [ˈbrʌslz]	Brüssel	
Brazil [brəˈzɪl]	Brasilien	

camper van [ˈkæmpə væn]	Wohnmobil	
cheap [tʃiːp]	billig	
clean [kliːn]	sauber	
beach [biːtʃ]	Strand	
on the beach [ɒn ðə ˈbiːtʃ]	am Strand	
all the time [ɔːl ðə ˈtaɪm]	die ganze Zeit, andauernd	
to **rain** [reɪn]	regnen	
to **stop** [stɒp]	aufhören	
all day [ɔːl ˈdeɪ]	den ganzen Tag lang	
4 **sb enjoys sth** [ɪnˈdʒɔɪz]	jdm gefällt etw	
somewhere [ˈsʌmweə]	irgendwo	
6 **Swiss** [swɪs]	Schweizer, schweizerisch	
partner [ˈpɑːtnə]	Lebensgefährte/-in, Partner/in	
to **book** [bʊk]	buchen, reservieren	
7 to **cook a meal** [ˌkʊk ə ˈmiːl]	kochen, eine Mahlzeit zubereiten	
9 to **be away** [bi əˈweɪ]	weg sein, verreist sein	
Hungary [ˈhʌŋgəri]	Ungarn	
relaxing [rɪˈlæksɪŋ]	erholsam, entspannend	
10 **Sweden** [ˈswiːdn]	Schweden	
EP4 **too big** [ˌtuː ˈbɪg]	zu groß	

UNIT 8   Where did you stay?

1 **apartment** [əˈpɑːtmənt]	Wohnung	
lake [leɪk]	See	
to **stay** [steɪ]	übernachten	
bed and breakfast [ˌbed ən ˈbrekfəst]	Frühstückspension, Zimmer mit Frühstück	
campsite [ˈkæmpsaɪt]	Campingplatz	
sea [siː]	Meer	
by the sea [baɪ ðə ˈsiː]	am Meer	
3 **about** [əˈbaʊt]	ungefähr	
did [dɪd]	*Simple past von* to do	
quiet [ˈkwaɪət]	ruhig	
mountain [ˈmaʊntən]	Berg	
expensive [ɪkˈspensɪv]	teuer	
to **walk** [wɔːk]	wandern, spazieren gehen	
to **go on holiday** [ˌgəʊ ɒn ˈhɒlədeɪ]	Urlaub machen, in den Urlaub fahren	
to **get away** [ˌget əˈweɪ]	wegkommen, verreisen	
around here [əˌraʊnd ˈhɪə]	hier in der Gegend	
to **rent sth** [rent]	(sich) etw mieten	
to **hire sth** [haɪə]	(sich) etw mieten	

How was your holiday?

How was your holiday?	Wie war Ihr/dein/euer Urlaub?
– Great, we were in …	– Toll, wir waren in …
We stayed in a quiet guesthouse / holiday flat	Wir haben in einer ruhigen Pension / Ferienwohnung gewohnt.
We booked a caravan at a campsite by the sea.	Wir haben einen Wohnwagen auf einem Campingplatz am Meer gebucht.
What was that like?	Wie war es (denn so)?
How about you?	Und Sie/du/ihr?

UNIT 9   We had a great time

to **have a great time** [həv ə ˌgreɪt ˈtaɪm]	sich blendend amüsieren, eine schöne Zeit (miteinander) verbringen	
had [hæd, həd]	*Simple past von* to have	
1 to **fly** [flaɪ]	fliegen	
3 **postcard** [ˈpəʊstkɑːd]	Postkarte	

flew [fluː] — Simple past von to fly
Geneva [dʒəˈniːvə] — Genf
came [keɪm] — Simple past von to come
by train [baɪ ˈtreɪn] — mit dem Zug
fondue [ˈfɒnduː] — Fondue
drank [dræŋk] — Simple past von to drink
waiter [ˈweɪtə] — Kellner
saw [sɔː] — Simple past von to see
sunset [ˈsʌnset] — Sonnenuntergang
boat [bəʊt] — Boot, Schiff
boat trip [ˈbəʊt trɪp] — Boots(rund)fahrt, Bootsausflug
storm [stɔːm] — Sturm, Unwetter
bought [bɔːt] — Simple past von to buy
tour [tʊə] — Rundgang, Führung
photograph [ˈfəʊtəɡrɑːf] — Foto
to take a photograph [ˌteɪk ə ˈfəʊtəɡrɑːf] — fotografieren, ein Foto machen
took [tʊk] — Simple past von to take
met [met] — Simple past von to meet
Love, [lʌv] — Alles Liebe, Herzliche Grüße
6 plane [pleɪn] — Flugzeug
9 opera [ˈɒprə] — Oper
9 opera house [ˈɒprə haʊs] — Oper, Opernhaus
10 city trip [ˈsɪti trɪp] — Städtereise
EP3 Warsaw [ˈwɔːsɔː] — Warschau
Spanish [ˈspænɪʃ] — spanisch

Writing a postcard

Dear/Hi… — Liebe(r) / Hallo …
Hello from … The weather's great. — Grüße aus … Das Wetter ist toll.
See you next week. — Bis nächste Woche.
Best wishes / Love … — Viele Grüße / Alles Liebe …

UNIT 10 Consolidation

1 review [rɪˈvjuː] — Bewertung, Rezension
bathroom [ˈbɑːθruːm] — Badezimmer, Bad
at first [ət ˈfɜːst] — zunächst, anfangs
toilet [ˈtɔɪlət] — Toilette
dirty [ˈdɜːti] — schmutzig, dreckig
handy [ˈhændi] — praktisch
sight [saɪt] — Sehenswürdigkeit
shower [ˈʃaʊə] — Dusche
to work [wɜːk] — funktionieren

service [ˈsɜːvɪs] — Bedienung, Service
to recommend sth [ˌrekəˈmend] — etw empfehlen
staff [stɑːf] — Personal
to move [muːv] — umziehen
view [vjuː] — Aussicht, Ausblick
connection [kəˈnekʃn] — Verbindung
complaint [kəmˈpleɪnt] — Beschwerde
to make a complaint [ˌmeɪk ə kəmˈpleɪnt] — sich beschweren
4 to fix sth [fɪks] — etw reparieren
5 sea view [ˈsiː vjuː] — Meerblick
7 to come back [ˌkʌm ˈbæk] — zurückkommen
9 Turkey [ˈtɜːki] — Türkei
10 call [kɔːl] — Telefonat, Anruf
to send sth [send] — etw abschicken
subject [ˈsʌbdʒɪkt] — (Brief usw.:) Betreff
holiday apartment [ˈhɒlədeɪ əpɑːtmənt] — Ferienwohnung
Best wishes, [ˌbest ˈwɪʃɪz] — Viele Grüße

Can you fix it?

It's me. The shower doesn't work. — Ich bin's. Die Dusche funktioniert nicht.
– I'm sorry. — – Das tut mir leid.
Can you fix it, please? — Können Sie das bitte reparieren?
– In ten minutes from now. Is that all right? — – Wir sind in zehn Minuten da. Wäre Ihnen das recht?

UNIT 11 How much is it?

1 underground [ˈʌndəɡraʊnd] — U-Bahn
to cycle [ˈsaɪkl] — (mit dem) Rad fahren, radeln
3 ticket [ˈtɪkɪt] — Fahrkarte, Fahrschein
train ticket [ˈtreɪn tɪkɪt] — Bahnfahrkarte
5 to remember sb/sth [rɪˈmembə] — sich an jdn/etw erinnern
to check [tʃek] — nachsehen
return ticket [rɪˌtɜːn ˈtɪkɪt] — (Hin- und) Rückfahrkarte
day return ticket [ˌdeɪ rɪˈtɜːn tɪkɪt] — Tagesrückfahrkarte

single ticket [ˌsɪŋɡl ˈtɪkɪt] — einfache Fahrkarte, Fahrkarte für einfache Fahrt

than [ðən] — (Vergleich:) als

to change trains [ˌtʃeɪndʒ ˈtreɪnz] — umsteigen

direct train [dəˈrekt treɪn] — durchgehender Zug (ohne Umsteigen)

travel card [ˈtrævl kɑːd] — Netzkarte, Zeitkarte

definitely [ˈdefɪnətli] — definitv, auf jeden Fall, ganz sicher

to collect sth [kəˈlekt] — etw abholen

machine [məˈʃiːn] — Automat

to arrive [əˈraɪv] — ankommen, eintreffen

platform [ˈplætfɔːm] — Bahnsteig, Gleis

6 **to leave** [liːv] — fahren, abfahren

9 **Spain** [speɪn] — Spanien

10 **announcement** [əˈnaʊnsmənt] — Durchsage

Attention please ... [əˈtenʃn pliːz] — Bitte beachten Sie: ...

platform change [ˈplætfɔːm tʃeɪndʒ] — Gleisänderung

11 **Italy** [ˈɪtəli] — Italien

ticket price [ˈtɪkɪt praɪs] — Fahrpreis

ticket office [ˈtɪkɪt ɒfɪs] — Fahrkartenschalter

passenger [ˈpæsɪndʒə] — Fahrgast

assistant [əˈsɪstənt] — Verkäufer/in

I'd like ... (= I would like ...) [ˌaɪd ˈlaɪk] — Ich hätte gern ...

Milan [mɪˈlæn] — Mailand

EP4 **Poland** [ˈpəʊlənd] — Polen

At the station

How much is a (return) ticket to..., please? — Wie viel kostet bitte eine (Rück-)Fahrkarte nach ...?

A day return ticket is ..., but a single is ... — Eine Tagesrückfahrkarte kostet ..., aber eine Einzelfahrkarte kostet ...

And we don't change trains? – No, it's a direct train. — Und wir steigen nicht um? – Nein, das ist ein durchgehender Zug.

It's the quickest and easiest way to travel to ... — Das ist der schnellste und einfachste Weg nach ...

Can we have two tickets, please? — Könnten wir bitte zwei Fahrkarten haben?

UNIT 12   It looks lovely!

1 to **try sth on** [ˌtraɪ ˈɒn] — etw anprobieren

dress [dres] — Kleid

department store [dɪˈpɑːtmənt stɔː] — Kaufhaus, Warenhaus

size [saɪz] — Größe

Just a minute, please. [ˌdʒʌst ə ˈmɪnɪt pliːz] — Einen Moment, bitte.

2 **jacket** [ˈdʒækɪt] — Jacke

3 **changing room** [ˈtʃeɪndʒɪŋ ruːm] — Umkleidekabine

short [ʃɔːt] — kurz

shoe [ʃuː] — Schuh

department [dɪˈpɑːtmənt] — Abteilung

comfortable [ˈkʌmftəbl] — bequem

worse [wɜːs] — schlimmer, schlechter

to spend [spend] — (Geld:) ausgeben

5 **worst** [wɜːst] — schlechteste/r/s, schlimmste/r/s

10 **purple** [ˈpɜːpl] — lila, violett

9 **to sell sth** [sel] — etw verkaufen

pair [peə] — Paar

a pair of ... [ə ˈpeər əv] — ein Paar ...

window [ˈwɪndəʊ] — Fenster, Schaufenster

blouse [blauz] — Bluse

10 **right here** [ˌraɪt ˈhɪə] — gleich hier

EP1 **gift** [gɪft] — Geschenk

EP3 **Cashmere** [ˈkæʃmɪə] — Kaschmir(wolle)

scarf [skɑːf] — Schal, Tuch

Shopping

Excuse me, can I try on this dress, please? — Entschuldigung, kann bitte ich dieses Kleid anprobieren?

– The changing room is right here. — Die Umkleidekabine ist gleich hier.

What size are you? — Welche Größe haben Sie/hast du/habt ihr?

Do I look OK in this? — Steht mir das einigermaßen?

It's better than ... — Das ist besser als ...

UNIT 13   I'd like a garden

1 **bedroom** [ˈbedruːm] — Schlafzimmer

balcony [ˈbælkəni] — Balkon

dining room Esszimmer
[ˈdaɪnɪŋ ruːm]
kitchen [ˈkɪtʃɪn] Küche
living room [ˈlɪvɪŋ ruːm] Wohnzimmer
2 **estate agent** Immobilienmakler/in
[ɪˈsteɪt eɪdʒənt]
flat BE [flæt] Wohnung
4 to **come in** [ˌkʌm ˈɪn] hereinkommen
bungalow [ˈbʌŋgələʊ] Bungalow
shower room Duschbad
[ˈʃaʊə ruːm]
own [əʊn] eigene/r/s
place [pleɪs] Haus, Wohnung
upstairs [ˌʌpˈsteəz] oben *(im Haus)*
downstairs [ˌdaʊnˈsteəz] unten *(im Haus)*
9 **lucky** [ˈlʌki] glücklich, Glücks-
to **share sth** [ʃeə] sich etw teilen
heating [ˈhiːtɪŋ] Heizung
central heating Zentralheizung
[ˌsentrəl ˈhiːtɪŋ]
10 **bath** [bɑːθ] Badewanne
S **ground floor** Erdgeschoss
[ˌgraʊnd ˈflɔː]
EP3 **beef** [biːf] Rindfleisch
EP4 **tuna fish** [ˈtjuːnə fɪʃ] Thunfisch
EP5 **pocket** [ˈpɒkɪt] (Hosen-, Jacken-)Tasche

Our house

We live in a bungalow /   Wir wohnen in einem
terraced house / (semi-)   Bungalow / Reihenhaus /
detached house /   Doppelhaus / Einfamili-
cottage and we...   enhaus / kleinen
                               Landhaus und wir ...
... have two bedrooms.   ... haben zwei
                               Schlafzimmer.
... don't have a garden.   ... haben keinen
... need a bigger place.   Garten.
                               ... brauchen eine größere
                               Wohnung / ein größeres
                               Haus / mehr Platz.

UNIT 14   I hate gardening

to **hate sth** [heɪt] etw überhaupt nicht
                        mögen, etw hassen
gardening [ˈgɑːdnɪŋ] Gartenarbeit
1 to **fish** [fɪʃ] angeln, fischen
to **bake** [beɪk] backen

2 **stairs** *pl* [steəz] Treppe
4 **neighbour** [ˈneɪbə] Nachbar/in
fast [fɑːst] schnell
bike [baɪk] Fahrrad
to **have a look (at sth)** sich etw ansehen
[həv ə ˈlʊk]
9 to **relax** [rɪˈlæks] sich erholen, sich
                          entspannen
to **chat to sb** [ˈtʃæt tə] sich mit jdm unterhalten,
                             mit jdm plaudern

Free time

I don't have much free   Ich habe nicht viel
time, but I love ...   Freizeit, aber ich mag ...
                           sehr gern.
Do you do any sport? –   Treiben Sie/treibst du/
I hate ...   treibt ihr irgendeine
                           Sportart? – Ich mag ...
                           überhaupt nicht.
I find ... relaxing.   Ich finde ... entspan-
                           nend.
Come on then!   Na los, auf geht's!

UNIT 15   Consolidation

1 **table** [ˈteɪbl] Tisch
chair [tʃeə] Sessel, Stuhl
desk [desk] Schreibtisch
bed [bed] Bett
lamp [læmp] Lampe
cupboard [ˈkʌbəd] Schrank
wardrobe [ˈwɔːdrəʊb] Kleiderschrank
furniture [ˈfɜːnɪtʃə] Möbel *pl*
2 to **compare sth (to sth)** etw (mit etw) vergleichen
[kəmˈpeə]
4 **carpet** [ˈkɑːpɪt] Teppich
at least [ət ˈliːst] wenigstens, zumindest,
                         mindestens
to **order** [ˈɔːdə] bestellen
store [stɔː] Laden, Geschäft
to **look at sth** [ˈlʊk ət] sich etw ansehen
6 to **move in** [ˌmuːv ˈɪn] einziehen
8 **waitress** [ˈweɪtrɪs] Kellnerin
9 **a five minutes' walk** fünf Minuten zu Fuß
[ə ˌfaɪv mɪnɪts ˈwɔːk]
to **sit** [sɪt] sitzen
to **have a meal** essen
[həv ə miːl]

rent [rent] Miete
per [pə] pro
R **likes and dislikes** *pl* Vorlieben und
[ˌlaɪks ən ˈdɪslaɪks] Abneigungen
advertisment Anzeige, Annonce
[ədˈvɜːtɪsmənt]

Furniture

We need a new ... Wir brauchen einen neuen/eine neue/ein neues ...

... bed ... Bett
... carpet ... Teppich
... chair/sofa ... Stuhl / Sessel / Sofa
... lamp ... Lampe
... desk/table ... Schreibtisch / Tisch
... TV ... Fernseher/ Fernsehapparat
... wardrobe ... Kleiderschrank

Bildquellen

Track List

Gesamtlänge: 1:41:31

Track	Exercise	Running Time
01	Copyright & Credits	01:02
Unit 1		
02	01	00:32
03	02	00:15
04	04	01:34
05	Facts & Fun	01:32
Unit 2		
06	01	00:38
07	02	00:26
08	04	01:07
09	05	00:19
10	07	01:42
11	Facts & Fun	01:48
12	Extra Practice 02	01:04
Unit 3		
13	01	00:30
14	03	01:18
15	10	01:26
16	Facts & Fun	01:43
Unit 4		
17	01	00:33
18	02	00:21
19	04	01:11
20	08	01:17
21	Facts & Fun	01:31
Unit 5		
22	01	00:55
23	06	00:28
24	08	00:51
Unit 6		
25	01	00:37
26	02	00:21
27	04	01:40
28	09	01:15
29	Facts & Fun	01:41
30	Extra Practice 06	01:22

Track	Exercise	Running Time
Unit 7		
31	01	00:20
32	03	01:41
33	07	00:48
34	09	00:31
35	10	01:23
36	Facts & Fun	02:00
37	Extra Practice 05	01:12
Unit 8		
38	01	00:32
39	03	01:41
40	09	01:20
41	Facts & Fun	01:39
42	Extra Practice 01	00:31
Unit 9		
43	01	00:46
44	03	01:58
45	09	00:38
46	Facts & Fun	01:52
Unit 10		
47	01	01:31
48	04	00:32
49	09	00:56
50	10	01:01
Unit 11		
51	01	00:40
52	03	00:22
53	05	02:00
54	10	01:26
55	Facts & Fun	02:05
56	Extra Practice 02	00:40
57	Extra Practice 03	00:45
Unit 12		
58	01	00:27
59	03	01:45
60	08	01:30
61	Facts & Fun	01:56
62	Extra Practice 02	00:39

Track	Exercise	Running Time
Unit 13		
63	01	00:44
64	02	00:23
65	04	01:26
66	09	00:56
67	Facts & Fun	01:38
Unit 14		
68	01	00:46
69	02	00:23
70	04	01:15
71	08	01:30
72	Facts & Fun	01:37
Unit 15		
73	03	01:35
74	08	00:40
75	09	01:42
Short Stories		
76	Story 1	02:56
77	Story 2	03:23
78	Story 3	03:01
79	Story 4	03:08
80	Story 5	02:58
81	Story 6	03:01

Studio:
Clarity Studio Berlin

Regie und Aufnahmeleitung:
Susanne Kreutzer

Tontechnik:
Gislinde Böhringer, Nathan Crowe

Sprecherinnen und Sprecher:
Sukhesh Arora, Malgorzata Dudley, Mala Ghedia, Elsa Giunipero, Imogen Guinipero, Melissa Holroyd, Melissa Jung, Susanne Kreutzer, Guda Koster, Angus McGruther, Christian Schmitz, Darren Smith, Tomas Spencer, Joshua Spriggs, Laura Wilkinson, Ian Wood.